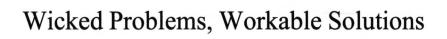

Wicked Problems, Workable Solutions

Also by Daniel Yankelovich

Toward Wiser Public Judgment. Nashville: Vanderbilt University Press, 2011. With Will Friedman.

Profit With Honor: The New Stage of Market Capitalism. New Haven: Yale University Press, 2007.

Uniting America: Restoring the Vital Center to American Democracy. Editor, with Norton Garfinkle. New Haven: Yale University Press, 2006.

The Magic of Dialogue: Transforming Conflict into Cooperation. New York: Simon & Schuster, 1999.

Beyond the Beltway: Engaging the Public in U.S. Foreign Policy. Editor, with I.M. Destler. New York: W.W. Norton and Company, 1994.

Coming to Public Judgment: Making Democracy Work in a Complex World. Syracuse: Syracuse University Press, 1991.

Starting with the People. Boston: Houghton Mifflin Company, 1988. With Sidney Harman.

The World at Work: An International Report on Jobs, Productivity and Human Values. Octagon Books, 1985.

New Rules: Searching for Self-fulfillment in a World Turned Upside Down. New York: Random House, 1981.

The New Morality: A Profile of American Youth in the Seventies. New York: McGraw-Hill, 1978.

Work, Productivity and Job Satisfaction. New York: Harcourt Brace, 1975. With Raymond A. Katzell and others.

Changing Values on Campus: Political and Personal Attitudes of Today's College Students. New York: Washington Square Press, 1973.

Ego and Instinct: The Psychoanalytic View of Human Nature-Revised. New York: Random House, 1969. With William Barrett.

Wicked Problems, Workable Solutions

Lessons from a Public Life

Daniel Yankelovich

ROWMAN & LITTLEFIELD
Lanham • Boulder • New York • London

Published by Rowman & Littlefield
A wholly owned subsidiary of The Rowman & Littlefield Publishing Group, Inc.
4501 Forbes Boulevard, Suite 200, Lanham, Maryland 20706
www.rowman.com

Unit A, Whitacre Mews, 26-34 Stannery Street, London SE11 4AB

British Library Cataloguing in Publication Information Available

Library of Congress Cataloging-in-Publication Data Available

ISBN 978-1-4422-4480-1 (cloth : alk. paper) -- 978-1-4422-4481-8 (electronic)

♾™ The paper used in this publication meets the minimum requirements of American
National Standard for Information Sciences Permanence of Paper for Printed Library
Materials, ANSI/NISO Z39.48-1992.

Printed in the United States of America

I dedicate this book to the thinkers who kept my interest in philosophy alive long after I had grown disillusioned with logic as a way of discovering the truths of living. They include Isaiah Berlin, Richard Rorty, Jurgen Habermas, Alfred North Whitehead, Hannah Arendt, Martha Nussbaum, William Barrett, and John Dewey.

Table of Contents

ACKNOWLEDGMENTS

I am grateful to the people who helped me at all stages of the book's development. For their help on how to structure the book so that its various parts held together as a single whole, I thank my friend Norton Garfinckle and my agent Ron Goldfarb.

For all of their helpful insights in reading parts of the draft I thank Leon Shapiro, Laurie Rosenblatt, Paul and Susan Drake, Jeff Elman, and Kathy Kilfara. And great appreciation to my niece, Fay, for her imaginative art.

For her moral support I am grateful to my beloved daughter, Nicole. Above all, for Laura, who not only edits with exquisite skill but who makes everything possible.

I

Elitism versus Democracy

Chapter One

Introduction: America's Wicked Problems

For almost forty years our economy has bred stagnant wages, long-term unemployment, huge disparities of wealth, and fewer escalators of social mobility.

This is without doubt a "Wicked Problem."

"Wicked Problems" share these characteristics:

- *There are no quick fixes.*
- *They are complex and multifaceted.*
- *Conventional methods (legislation, regulation, money, power, technology) don't —and can't—solve them.*
- *Solutions depend on how the problem is framed.*
- *Every wicked problem is essentially novel and unique.*

In recent years, not only our economy, but also our culture and our national gift for compromise and practical problem solving have taken a big hit.

Our nation seems to have lost its traditional knack for pragmatic problem solving. Americans feel our society is becoming ever more unfair and unresponsive. Important issues pile up unattended; public mistrust of our institutions grows more entrenched.

On the cultural front, the sharp distinction between what is morally right and what is merely legal—formerly a foundational ethic of our culture—has grown blurry. Many people rationalize their behavior by saying, "I didn't break the law so I couldn't have done anything wrong."

Cultures are supposed to provide guidance for individuals on what really matters in life. American culture used to be rigid and conformist, but at least our cultural values were clear and compelling. This is no longer the case. The cultural revolution launched in the 1960s lurched too violently toward extreme individualism. It may take another generation or two to restore the sense of community and balance we need for our society to function successfully.

Perceptive critics characterize our troubled era in a variety of ways. Social critic Matt Miller observes that all current measures of a good society are moving in the *wrong direction*—wages, school rankings, college costs, health care costs, poverty rates, job opportunities, and so forth. [1]

Journalist Peggy Noonan (*Wall Street Journal*) laments, "The great unstated question of today: Can America come back, reclaim her old spirit, confidence and joy, can we make things again, build them, grow, create, push out into the new? And here I think: Oh dear."[2]

New Yorker writer George Packer names his book of contemporary American lives *The Unwinding*. Packer perceives significant deterioration of the power of our mores to bind us together as a civilization. Optimistically, however, he observes that "there have been unwindings every generation or two and out of each came a new cohesion."[3]

I share Packer's hopeful assumption that a new cohesion will eventually emerge. But I don't think it's going to happen quickly or automatically. Before we can pull ourselves together once again, we may have to live through years of downward twists and turns, and it will take more than luck to see us through.

How did all this happen?

In the early days of the cultural revolution that incubated on the nation's college campuses in the 1960s, the ardent young students who were arguing for change visualized a new culture that balanced individual autonomy with concern for the common good. They never imagined that our culture would impulsively seize on the individual autonomy part of the balance and push concern with the common good—what the Romans called the *res publica*—into the background.

In its present lopsided state, our culture's norms have lost their former authority. Now we have to learn to live our lives without expecting much guidance from the culture.

Perhaps most disturbing of all, our political leaders no longer feel the need to engage the public in shaping policies that directly impact people's lives.

For example, neither President Obama nor President Clinton—both champions of democracy—made an effort to engage the public in formulating their new health care policies or even to explain to Americans how the policies were supposed to work. They worked instead with technical experts, insurance companies, and physician organizations, who all had their own agendas to pursue.

When our leaders avoid public engagement, we no longer have a democracy of, by, and for the people. Instead we have a government of elites shaping policies *for* the people, but without their active participation.

The combined impact of this jumble of changes finds today's America in a troubling situation and the American public in a troubled state of mind. The majority has concluded that "the country is on the wrong track." And we seem clueless about how to get back on track. (The wrong track metaphor may be much too mild a euphemism for the deep hole we are digging for ourselves.)

The thesis of this book is that with all the wicked problems the nation faces, it will be difficult to get back on track without a more thoughtful, more fully engaged public, and without a more public-minded philosophy than now prevails. Today's public feels powerless, mistrustful, inattentive, and disengaged. This makes our wicked problems harder to resolve.

In politics, abuse breeds abuse. If our leaders and elites abuse powers that rightly belong to the people, then we should not be surprised when we get an angry, nonrational, equally abusive response from the public.

We see this nonrational scenario playing out all over the world—in Ukraine, Turkey, Iraq, Libya, Pakistan, Bangladesh, Thailand, and so on. The public in these countries are venting their anger and frustration in the public square, but without having thought through practical solutions to their grievances.

In the United States, we haven't reached this tipping point yet, but we inevitably will unless we find some way to give Americans as citizens more say over their lives and governance.

In this book I want to share with readers what I've learned from more than sixty years of studying and monitoring public opinion. I've learned that public thoughtfulness and pragmatic practicality *can* prevail and *can* be responsive to leadership. I've learned that Americans are deeply concerned about their country and willing to sacrifice for it and care for it in profound ways. I've learned that sound public judgment *can* be cultivated into a force for thoughtful pragmatism and deliberation.

Such conditions do not come about by accident. They need to be nourished. Our submerged public wisdom can help the nation to navigate through the wicked problems that have descended on us like a thick, wet fog.

The most practical strategy, even though it may at first sound impractical, is to arm a critical mass of Americans with a distinctive philosophy that has a central role for what used to be called "civic virtue"—giving priority to the well-being of the larger society over the wilder excesses of individualism.

We live in a profoundly technological civilization. Science and technology have contributed enormously to the well-being of our society and will continue to do so. But technology by itself cannot address—and solve—the wicked problems that confront us. We need a counterbalance to technology; we need better philosophies for living.

I don't mean the kind of technical philosophies that are bottled up in our colleges and universities. I mean philosophies for living that take full advantage of all that we have learned in recent years about human cognition, co-evolution, culture, and conflict resolution.

In the coming decades

- We will need to upgrade the public's role in our democracy. Americans must become as effective as citizens as they are as consumers.
- We will need to restore greater fairness to our system of capitalism, so that it is once again democracy-friendly.
- We will need to rebuild the moral authority of our culture and provide individuals with better tools for making life's existential decisions.

These are huge tasks. But they can be accomplished if we are brave enough and smart enough.

Philosophy is our civilization's most ancient discipline. It meets a basic human need. But the old wine (wisdom) now has to be poured into new bottles.

Chapter Two

Retrofitting the Plumbing of Democracy

I learned an important lesson about American life when my career shifted from studying Americans as consumers to studying Americans as citizen participants in our democracy.

I had begun my career in the marketing research field, analyzing how people make up their minds as consumers. I studied the full range of consumer decision making from major life commitments (buying a home) to trivial decisions (choosing one brand of coffee over another).

As my focus shifted from consumer behavior to citizen behavior, I began to study how Americans feel about home, family, religion, and country. I gradually specialized in the analysis of how Americans make up their minds about political and societal issues: how they judge the qualifications of political candidates, how they reach their decisions on the role of government, health care, immigration, K–12 education reform, initiatives to reduce inequality, and so forth.

I am constantly impressed by how much more comfortable Americans are about performing their role as consumers than as citizens. As consumers, they pay relatively careful attention to their buying decisions; they are aware of key facts about their choices, and they are thoughtful and deliberative, having spent time and effort working through the important pros and cons.

For the large and successful companies that were my firm's clients, companies like Ford and General Electric, the stakes were often huge. All of them held the consumer in great respect. I realized how highly they regarded their customers when my research shifted to controversial social and political issues. Public policy makers proved far more dismissive of public attitudes than business executives, and far less interested in the public's real concerns.

Business executives learn, often the hard way, that consumers are not easily manipulated. Americans pay close attention to differences in prices and product features; they respond quickly to competitive initiatives, and in general, they are readily engaged in shopping and purchase behavior.

Not so when it comes to their role as citizens. On many of the fateful issues of the day, the public's attention span has proven short; people are ignorant of the most basic facts; they do not take much effort to work through their own wishful thinking and are reluctant to confront and resolve issues that involve painful trade-offs.

When shopping for products, Americans feel they are in the driver's seat. They know that companies are obliged to take their views and habits into account if they wish to thrive.

On social and policy issues, the opposite mind-set prevails. Average Americans feel their views really don't count, so they see no reason to commit serious time and effort to them. Public engagement is lacking on issues where the public voice is almost wholly ineffectual.

The differences in the dynamics of being a consumer and being a citizen are dramatic and vivid; they are not subtle. Americans are fully engaged as consumers; they are not fully engaged as citizens.

My experience with the health care issue dramatized for me the extent to which our system of governance bypasses public participation.

Back in the Clinton administration, Hillary Clinton sought to extend health care to many more Americans. But her health care plan was a complex Rube Goldberg contraption designed by policy wonks, with no effective public input.

At the time, I happened to be studying American attitudes toward health care. I came to feel I was living in two different universes. One was the highly abstract world of Ms. Clinton's chief health care adviser, Ira Magaziner, who had a "gift" for complicating issues.

The other was the world of the practical-minded American public who were largely satisfied with the insurance their employers provided and were almost totally unaware of the costs associated with their health care.

I made an effort to alert Ms. Clinton to the reality that if and when the public came to fully understand Ira Magaziner's fantasy, they would turn against the plan. Ms. Clinton was courteous and attentive, but it was too late to make significant changes.

With this serious error of attempting to shape a health care policy without consulting the public, I was sure that the next reform-minded president would pay heed and not repeat the same mistake.

How wrong I turned out to be! The Affordable Health Care Act (Obama-Care) had plenty of insurance company input. But it had no input from the American public.

Even when the plan was completed, and its website proved to be a disaster, the Obama administration didn't really try to explain it to the public. Hard to believe, but the resistance of our political leaders to engaging the public on important issues is a powerful obstacle to the functioning of our democracy.

The reasons public input is largely absent are not obvious. But they are quickly revealed once one digs into the plumbing of how the public makes up its mind and the role of the media in that process.

I am a great admirer of America's news media. For many years I was closely associated with two highly influential media companies—*The New York Times* and *TIME* magazine.[1] The *NY Times*/Yankelovich poll of national public opinion is still operating as the *NY Times*/CBS poll. For *TIME* magazine, I created the *TIME* Magazine/Yankelovich poll.

In more recent years, I've come to the conclusion that the news media do a very one-sided job. They are great when it comes to raising the public's consciousness about an issue—the health care controversy or illegal immigration or American students falling behind students from other nations and so on. But the media don't like to go on investigating issues that are no longer "news" because this is how they define their identity—as news organizations.

This one-sidedness hides a serious vacuum from public scrutiny: headline news receives an enormous amount of media attention. But other aspects of issues are neglected. The difficult trade-offs, emotional conflicts, and detailed pros and cons of issues receive scant news media attention. In my experience, the media gets tired of an issue once it is no longer news *often at precisely the moment the public is beginning to focus on it.*

Having devoted decades of my life to this "plumbing" side of our democracy, I know what the problem is, even if it is almost impossible to fix.

Part of the problem is that the media are committed to an oversimplified model of how people make up their minds. The media assume that once people have the relevant facts, they will immediately make up their minds about an issue. In fact, on complex issues the public's learning curve requires weeks, months, years, and even decades to find resolution (e.g., gay rights, the health hazards of cigarette smoking, equal pay for women).

The media exaggerate the role that information plays in the public's decision making. They quote Thomas Jefferson's dictum that an informed public is indispensable to democracy. In Jefferson's time, however, being well-informed included bringing sound judgment to bear as well as accurate facts. Today, being well informed merely means knowing the facts of the case—the "daily news."

The media are in the news and entertainment businesses. They don't like being told that more information by itself does little to help people come to judgment—and sometimes even does the opposite!

Chapter Three

A Plea for Adaptive Sanity

We Americans are most comfortable when we can solve a problem with a technical fix or by passing a law or by throwing money at it. But it is highly unlikely that such conventional types of fixes will, by themselves, succeed with the wicked problems we face.

Nothing less than a new multidimensional, distinctively American philosophy of life can succeed in revitalizing our society and addressing our wicked problems.

I have deliberately used the term "philosophy of life" rather than more familiar and socially acceptable terms, such as "world view" or "system of beliefs" or "ideology." In our era of high tech and big data, we no longer pay much attention to philosophies of life. They seem old-fashioned, relics of eras past, fit only for museum-like isolation in our colleges and universities. In the present context, however, no other term will do. I am not talking about a new ideology or general constellation of cultural values and beliefs. I am talking specifically about a *philosophy for living*.

I emphatically do not mean a *philosophy for scholars*. I mean a *philosophy for living for average Americans*.

"Philosophy for scholars" connotes the academic discipline of philosophy as taught in our colleges and universities. It features subjects such as epistemology (the theory of knowledge), logic, metaphysics, and the history of philosophy. Academic philosophy doesn't pretend to offer its followers much practical guidance on how to live their lives.

By "philosophy for living" I mean something quite different. I mean the assortment of principles and skills for living that individuals acquire from a great variety of sources—parental guidance, religious beliefs, cultural norms, personal experience, friends, mentors, literature, and the vicissitudes of life.

Strong philosophies for living have several essential features. They focus on ultimate values—the values that make life most worth living. They apply will, skill, and determination to putting first things first—to giving priority in their own lives to the values and activities that count most in living. And they seek to enhance sound judgment and avoid distorted thinking.

This sort of philosophy for living is a form of *adaptive sanity*.

As an example, in the first few months of his papacy, Pope Francis chided his followers for being obsessed with matters of secondary importance (such as gay marriage) at the expense of neglecting the fundamentals of Christianity: faith, charity, prayer. In doing so, he was making a philosophical plea to the community of Catholics—a plea to put first things first, and to look to their faith in the context of what is most urgent and important.

I am making a plea, then, for millions of average Americans to develop habits of thought and feelings they choose consciously that will lead to a new wave of vibrant and pragmatic philosophies of life.

The process of creating such a philosophy enriches one's own life and is, amazingly and deeply, *fun*: a joy to do.

When large numbers of Americans choose to do so, together we can install a deep layer of thought between our problem-ridden culture and our individual lives. This layer of thought will be the heritage we will leave for future generations.

Why should nurturing a more philosophy-of-living-minded public be the method of choice for repairing deep structural flaws in our culture and systems of governance? How might an individual's philosophy for living substitute for strong cultural norms as a guide to the best way to live one's life? Why is this the strategy of choice, rather than relying exclusively on specific economic and political policies and programs?

The answers turn out to be compelling.

Consider our system of democracy's failure to engage the public. Could it be that the reason our leaders, even those most committed to democracy, avoid doing so is their own bad experience in trying to engage the public?

In formats such as town hall meetings or forums open to the public, our leaders are often overwhelmed by great waves of mindless, raw opinion and raw emotion from the attending crowds. Many such leaders have learned that (at least in these formats), the public rarely seems willing to devote the time, thought, effort, attention span, and objectivity needed for serious deliberation of issues as complex as health care or foreign policy, or even the survival of the planet. It takes two to dance. Even the leaders who are prepared to engage cannot do so without public responsiveness.

If, however, a large and active part of the public brought a thoughtful philosophy of life to the engagement, the goal of sound public judgment would become more familiar, and public discussion more likely to achieve this goal.

The American heritage of a stable and cherished democracy built up over several hundred years is too valuable to waste through neglect. Armed with a new philosophy of life, more Americans would assign a high priority to public participation and engagement. A distinctively American philosophy for living would, inevitably, give new life to democratic self-governance.

Similar considerations apply to our social morality. A public without a philosophy for living is more likely to feel itself helpless in the face of mistrust and perceived injustice. That feeling of helplessness results in erosion of norms, and in passive acceptance of fate: "*Whatever . . .* "

Even when it comes to the economy, which can be a highly technical subject, the changes needed to create more equality of opportunity require the engagement of a thoughtful public who put first things first.

The task of restoring our system of capitalism to serve the people in all economic classes rather than primarily those on the top rungs of the ladder is much more a matter of political will than it is of technical economic expertise. A preference for a fair society with greater equality of opportunity is a philosophical preference, not an economic one.

What we need, then, each of us, is a philosophy that provides guidance both to individuals on how to live their personal lives, and to society on how to correct the wicked flaws that have developed over the past two generations.

Chapter Four

Four Wrong Turns

Developing a new cohesion, as individuals and as a society, requires coping with four trends that are destructive to our lives today.

THE TREND AWAY FROM DEMOCRATIC-FRIENDLY CAPITALISM

A major source of the current "unwinding" is an inadvertent, unintended shift in our economy. Starting in the 1970s, our economy gradually evolved toward a less democracy-friendly form of capitalism. Ever since, we have been edging away from the form of capitalism that is most compatible with political democracy.

In the decades following WWII, we became accustomed to the "rising tide raises all boats" form of capitalism—the most democratic of its forms. This is when economic growth benefits the vast majority of the public. Income levels rise for all demographic groups. Political stability prevails.

Up to recently, our giant corporations could be profitable only if a great many consumers had rising incomes to spend on their products and services. But in the recent past, companies have learned to become profitable *without* spreading the wealth throughout the society.

Under this new form of undemocratic capitalism, companies invest in technology. They improve their bottom line mainly by cutting labor costs, in however brutal a manner.

The French economist Thomas Piketty makes this point on the very first page of his best-selling book, *Capital in the Twenty-First Century*. He writes, "When the rate of return on capital exceeds the rate of growth of output and income . . . capitalism automatically generates arbitrary and unsustainable inequalities that radically undermine the meritocratic values on which demo-

15

cratic societies are based." Piketty calls this shift away from democracy-friendly capitalism "patrimonial capitalism"—a shift that sharply favors inherited wealth.[1]

What this means for the majority of Americans is that hard work, skill acquisition, and abiding by the rules are not rewarded as responsively as in the post–World War II period. Tens of millions of people have found their wages stagnant, and millions more remain unemployed or underemployed.

Clearly, if only those at the top of the income scale benefit from growth, this emerging form of capitalism can prove politically untenable in a nation with our democratic traditions.

Of course, there are many forms of world capitalism that are not consistent with democracy: for example, China's form of centralized capitalism or Russian and Ukrainian crony capitalism. In these forms, the rising tide raises only the biggest boats and political stability is constantly threatened. This is not an outcome most Americans desire to see in a nation committed to "liberty and justice for all."

It is plutocracy rather than democracy.

GROWTH OF INEQUALITY OF OPPORTUNITY

A second cause of the unwinding is closely related to the move away from democratic capitalism. It is the growing perception that we are ceasing to be a land of opportunity.

Those at the top are, indeed, doing extremely well. But incomes at all other levels, especially at the bottom, are stagnant or declining. It has become a truism that the American middle class is being hollowed out. The result is a rising tide of envy and distrust that we have largely escaped in the past.

In his 2014 State of the Union address, President Obama labeled inequality of opportunity and declining social mobility as the "defining challenge of our times" and proclaimed, "We must reverse these trends."

The "tide that raises all boats" form of capitalism has been generally accepted in the United States because average Americans are not opposed in principle to inequalities of income. Indeed, the vast majority of Americans endorses and legitimizes the inevitable inequalities of capitalism. But they do so with one indispensable qualification: capitalism works for the majority of Americans as long as—and only as long as—self-improvement and advancement are available to all who are willing to play by the rules. The point of view of the average American is this: "I don't care how much those at the top earn, as long as I have a fair chance to improve life for myself and my family."

This is an essential feature of our nation's social contract.

As long as it is observed, our political stability is safe, whatever other problems we may confront. My long experience conducting and interpreting public opinion polls tells me that if equality of opportunity continues to erode, extremist political movements will arise, shredding our social contract and making polarization far more extreme than it is today.

ERODING ETHICAL NORMS

The third form of unwinding relates to *non*economic cultural forces. Economies don't operate in a vacuum; their strengths and weaknesses depend on the larger political/ethical context of the society of which they are a part.

This is a truth that the founders of capitalist theory, most notably Adam Smith, fully recognized. Smith distinguished between *enlightened* and *unenlightened* capitalism. Capitalism is enlightened when those who practice it bring to bear an ethical concern for others. Smith labeled this concern "moral sympathy," which he thought to be hard-wired into human nature.

We use different language today but the ethical context is the same. Our giant corporations are expected to care for all of their constituents—employees, customers, shareholders, suppliers, and the larger community in which they operate. This form of caring is called an *ethic of stewardship*: that is, the company's top executives regard themselves as stewards of an enterprise that exists to serve others, not just its stockholders.

Without such an ethic, companies and individuals become exploitative; they abuse their power for short-term gain at the expense of those they purportedly serve. Our great financial institutions, our most trusted banks and investment companies, were caught in this frenzy of uncaring, unethical, short-term, manipulative thinking that led to the Great Recession of 2007–2008.

It was this sort of behavior that memorably caused Goldman Sachs to be compared to a giant vampire squid squeezing the life out of everything it touched.

The disastrous structural changes in our form of capitalism have coincided with a deteriorating social ethic of caring for others. We appear to be living through a period of general decline in ethical norms.

Sociologists refer to this phenomenon as *anomie*—a state of normlessness. Such periods are not "black swans" that happen only once every few centuries; they are normal occurrences that break out in all cultures at one time or another. We are living through one of these bad patches today here in the United States.

One sign of moral decline is an increasing frequency of over-the-top behavior by law-abiding citizens. Average citizens engaging in bizarre and deviant behavior is a danger signal of something morally amiss in the larger society.

For example, our nation's colleges are experiencing steady annual increases in student rapes. The college rape rate is now 20 percent—one out of five students are victims of a crime that once used to invoke the death penalty. The president of the United States cited this statistic as one of his major worries.[2]

Our military services—the navy, army, and air force—are all currently caught up in a series of scandals that has the secretary of defense worried about our moral character and courage.

On the civilian front, an ever growing of number of congressmen and other government officials are being caught in sexual misconduct.

Weirdest, and to my mind most worrisome, is the "Texting Incident." In a movie theater just outside of Tampa, Florida, a seventy-one-year-old retired police captain shot and killed a younger man—a total stranger—because he wouldn't stop texting while the movie previews were playing. The victim had stubbornly refused to heed the posted rules that texting was not permitted when the lights were off. He wanted to text, and nothing was going to stop him.

The retired police captain wanted him to stop texting, and nothing was going to stop *him*. Hence, the confrontation. *Two ordinary law-abiding citizens allowed their own willfulness to override the most elementary norms of civilized society, resulting in violence and tragedy.*

This is an extreme example of over-the-top individualism—people sweeping aside social norms that interfere with their own desires. Ordinary citizens are crossing the line, oblivious to the moral norms that have prevailed in most of our history since we became a nation.

THE LOSS OF SHARED FRAMEWORKS

A fourth source of the unwinding is the steady increase of specialization in our society. Excessive specialization is proving to be highly destructive of the shared frameworks needed to maintain a minimum of cohesion in our society.

As citizens, we need to keep the big picture in mind at all times; otherwise we lose perspective. But specialization inevitably works in the opposite direction: specialization breeds an ever more narrow focus, with each specialty spawning litters of subspecialties. While this trend may lead to special knowledge, it blocks out the big picture.

We live in an era of technological exuberance. Our lives have been transformed, mostly for the good, by the explosion of science-driven innovations.

Our ever more specialized world buys us disease-freer lives, superior com-munications, and greater convenience.

But these life enhancements come at a cost. Specialization makes it hard to maintain a common overview. If we see events through the lens of special-ists, and if specialists proliferate, society ends up with a clash of views rather than a unified coherent vision.

We certainly don't want to reverse the specialization trend. American civilization gains enormous benefits from specialization in the sciences and professions. We need to retain these benefits without reaching a tipping point where its drawbacks take over. An explicit philosophy-of-life outlook would help us to keep the whole elephant in mind at all times while simultaneously focusing on its specialized parts.

Chapter Five

Why We Can't Rely on Our Culture

Up to a generation or so ago, the findings of public opinion polls reflected a long-established pattern of American life. Though a majority of the public may have believed that the nation as a whole had wandered down the wrong path, most Americans felt optimistic about their own and their children's future. Almost universally, Americans believed their children would be better off than themselves, and they themselves were improving their own lot in life.

Now, however, that familiar pattern no longer holds. Polls show that Americans are apprehensive about their children's future. And they are less self-confident about their own.

I had a privileged view of this particular unwinding as it began in the 1960s and then proceeded in later decades to overtake the nation. My business research firm (Yankelovich, Skelly, and White) was given the opportunity to document the social movements that were just starting to challenge our nation's values and moral norms—the woman's movement, the civil rights movement, the environmental movement, the consumer movement, and the youth movement.

It's hard to imagine how conformist and conventional our society was in the 1950s. The culture's message to men and women was blunt and unqualified. Men were expected to get married, have children, work hard, make a comfortable living, climb the socioeconomic ladder, and serve as heads of their households.

A "real woman" was expected to subordinate any career aspirations she might have to her husband's. Raising a family was her main role in life, one that demanded major sacrifices from her, which she was obliged to make.

From the 1960s until the present decade, my firm conducted annual surveys of the public as the values of the 1960s spread to the population at large.

At first, the new values affected only a tiny minority of people, but by the mid-1970s and 1980s they had transformed the lives of more than four out of five Americans!

Our tracking studies over the past half-century record a genuine cultural revolution that has transformed our traditional core values on marriage, family, work, sex, leisure, health, social status, the environment, technology, race, social morality, diversity, self-expressiveness, citizen rights, and the importance of sacrificing for others.

Cultural revolutions are rare events in the history of nations, and their consequences can be long lasting. It is now the second decade of the twenty-first century and the effects of the cultural revolution that started in the 1960s continue to unfold, with mixed results, some positive, others less so.

Our society has grown far less prejudiced. Both men and women are freer than they were in the past to seek their own personal self-fulfillment. There are many fewer constraints on self-expressiveness.

On the other hand, individual satisfaction has come to trump concern for communal well-being. The desires of the self are pursued with blurred ethical guidelines. Families have become less stable. Social mobility as a reward for hard work can no longer be taken for granted.

These cultural changes have created a number of bewildering dilemmas for average Americans, especially when they take the form of "existential choices"—the fundamental life choices that all of us confront in one form or another.

Here are some of the kinds of choices that arise in our own cultural era for many middle-class individuals:

Whether to leave a marriage that may no longer be flourishing.

Whether to accept a cut in pay to avoid unemployment.

Whether a man should readily accept the role of a house-husband to permit his wife to pursue a demanding career that means a lot to her.

Whether a woman should sacrifice important aspects of self for family, career, or others.

Whether to work primarily for money or to pursue one's nonmonetary interests.

Whether to take ethical shortcuts in pursuit of your own desires.

Whether to abandon a lucrative and successful career when some other interest beckons.

In the past, a variety of institutions provided guidance for these sorts of existential choices. You could turn to your religious faith and the judgment of priests, ministers, imams, and rabbis. You could listen to your parents and other authority figures. You could adhere to the dominant norms of the culture. You could turn to self-help gurus. You could seek therapy. You could search for guidance in the writings of the great philosophers.

All of these sources of guidance still exist, and all of them continue to function for some people. But they have become riddled with ambiguities. In our era of unfettered individualism, you are thrown back on your own resources and judgment.

Chapter Six

Straight and Crooked Thinking

We are living in an era when crooked thinking is all too prevalent. Crooked thinking is distorted thinking, limited thinking, misdirected thinking. A sound pragmatic philosophy for living would hone one's everyday skills in distinguishing between straight and crooked thinking.

Some examples:

- The investment adviser loses a client. In his mind, he sees his client as an aging, unsophisticated widower and assumes that he can't afford to take any risks with his savings. Without asking further "invasive" questions, he invests his client's money ultraconservatively—preserving his capital but barely increasing it. In fact, the client has adequate income for himself, and so is prepared to take risks. The adviser's unexplored assumption turned out to be wrong, costing him a promising client. Crooked thinking.
- The surgeon makes an incorrect diagnosis. She is trained in pattern recognition and believes all hoofbeats denote horses. Thus, she fails to detect the subtle and lethal variation in the familiar pattern the patient presented. The patient dies. Crooked thinking.
- The teacher holds low expectations about the capacity of his class to learn science. He reviews the same basic materials every day, day after day. When his students respond with inattention and misbehavior, he takes it as confirmation of his assumption. Several of the brightest kids drop out of school, citing boredom and resentment. Crooked thinking.

All three professionals feel bad about their outcomes, but fail to realize that it was anything other than bad luck. A fluke. This assumption does not change their thinking; it merely confirms for them the inevitability of "bad luck."

These are common, everyday life mistakes of thought. They occur in countless variations. They seem inescapable, but they are not. They are errors in philosophical thinking. Our society is bogged down in this sort of crooked thinking. We have become philosophy-challenged—a nation full of smart people making dumb mistakes, feeling bad about them, and making them again. And again.

It is much more difficult to think straight than one might presume. Crooked thinking is, apparently, an inherent feature of the human mind. Cognitive psychologist Daniel Kahneman recently won a Nobel Prize for his research demonstrating that we are inherently error-prone creatures who cling passionately to our biases and our errors of judgment.

Kahneman's research challenges the assumption that the human mind is rational and logical. Instead, he concludes that our minds are prone to systemic error and are led astray by the inherent "design of the machinery of cognition."

Along with many other scientists, he discovers that most thinking is unconscious. It's a lot harder to recognize unconscious distortions in thinking than conscious ones.[1]

Crooked thinking rooted in unconscious processes can take many different forms. One of the most common is *groupthink*—the shared beliefs of insiders in the same community, company, or profession. At any one time, because of groupthink, most of those who manage our society are not thinking straight about matters of the utmost importance. Just glance at our political parties, our government, our banks and other financial institutions, our schools, our health care, our criminal justice system.

One of the most consequential forms of crooked thinking is the failure to develop the will and the skill needed to set priorities for one's life. Setting priorities requires the ability to distinguish between more important and less important values. Developing this one philosophical skill could, by itself, help to restore adaptive sanity to American society.

Another all-pervasive form of crooked thinking in today's America is failure to seek out and make explicit the tacit frameworks and assumptions that underlie the major areas of specialization. Professional practices in business, economics, medicine, law, education, politics, and science all have tacit frameworks that collide with each other and make it difficult for us to understand and cooperate with each other. Each religion has a tacit framework along with its formal one, and the tacit one is rarely discussed.

These three forms of cognitive distortion—groupthink, an inability to prioritize, and the assumptions made by hidden frameworks—underlie a variety of social problems in our nation, all of them involving widespread mistrust: Americans pitted against other Americans.

Examples of mistrust and imbalance in priorities are everywhere you look:

- Trust in our core American value—a level playing field with equal opportunity—has been badly eroded over the past four decades.
- Large numbers of Americans don't trust the government and are fearful that their country is being taken away from them. They react with fierce partisan resentment, creating destructive polarization in our politics.
- Our K–12 education system flounders in well-meaning but ineffectual reforms, breeding mistrust on all sides.
- The older generation's mandatory entitlements threaten the future well-being of the nation's youth, creating generational mistrust.
- The dangers of climate change mount, but widespread mistrust of science, among other factors, is preventing remedial action.

Every one of these issues calls for adaptive sanity to restore balance and perspective to our politics and national life. Both as individuals and as a society, we must revive the habit of philosophical thinking in daily life rather than locking it away in academic settings.

There is a powerful *feelings* dimension to philosophy as well as a thinking dimension. On the feelings side, philosophy helps us to make the best choices at life's crossroads and to understand the self well enough to pursue a meaningful life. The feeling aspect of philosophy is the ability *to see oneself* in varied contexts and to open oneself to new ways of thinking and responding.

The late philosopher Robert Nozick observed that most of us live our lives on automatic pilot, unthinkingly following goals we developed in childhood. Living the examined life permits us to escape these unnecessary limits and to conceive of our lives in a broader context.

When you follow the examined life, you build a self-portrait that encompasses your personal emotional, moral, and spiritual experiences as well as your more formal and objective thoughts. The self-portrait thus developed encompasses the great issues: how to live the good life, why wisdom is so highly valued, and how love can change the self. Reflecting on these sorts of questions is an essential part of the examined life.[2]

I have incorporated into my own philosophy of life an ethical concern with "stewardship"—the commitment to caring for others toward whom you feel a direct or indirect responsibility. Growing up as a poor boy in Boston, I was the frequent beneficiary of this stewardship commitment. I believe this form of caring for others is a profound aspect of our evolutionary heritage.

Chapter Seven

Caring and Stewardship

One of my firm's early market research studies highlights a memorable example of stewardship. The trade association for the supermarket industry had hired our firm to conduct research among both unionized and nonunion supermarkets.

One nonunion supermarket chain towered above the others in customer and employee satisfaction. It was the Publix chain of supermarkets in Florida. The employees we interviewed rhapsodized about Publix's CEO, a man named George Jenkins. To my surprise many of Publix's customers knew his name and praised his performance.

In speaking of Mr. Jenkins, employees kept repeating one particular phrase. A clerk would recount something Mr. Jenkins had done for him or her and would then add in wonder, "He didn't have to do that." This phrase cropped up in interview after interview.

I soon began to understand why.

Just one example will suffice: after a checkout clerk's husband had been hospitalized, Mr. Jenkins gave her ample time off to care for him and also personally visited him in the hospital.

The employee was grateful but not surprised. It was Jenkins's *second* visit to the hospitalized husband that won her astonished praise. One visit might be expected in keeping with Jenkins's code of caring. But a second hospital visit. Amazing! *He didn't have to do that.*

Publix was not unionized because no one felt that a union was needed to look out for employee interests as long as Mr. Jenkins was in charge. Time and again, Mr. Jenkins would surpass even his own generous stewardship code of ethics and win the supreme accolade: "He didn't have to do that."

Today large parts of our economic system are failing to observe the ethic of caring and stewardship they must have to continue to thrive.

We heap outlandish rewards on our business leaders for adhering to a terrible doctrine known as "shareholder value," which explicitly states that *shareholder* interests take priority over the interests of *all other stakeholders*—employees, customers, environmental concerns, the community at large.

Adam Smith and other founders of modern capitalism lauded "*enlightened* self-interest." The profit-maximizing doctrines favored by many of our financial institutions represent *un*enlightened self-interest in its crassest form.

In the midst of the banking crisis, I wrote a book with the title *Profit with Honor*. I deliberately used the out-of-fashion word "honor" to underscore how far our culture has wandered away from norms that support ethical bonds and obligations to others. Today, honor is given to those who are paid vast sums of money for activities that often have little redeeming social or economic value.

Most observers acknowledge that capitalism creates inequalities. This is a trade-off that most Americans willingly accept, despite the high value we place on equality. To reconcile the conflicting pulls of freedom and equality, Americans have settled on the principle of *equality of opportunity* as the underlying core value of democratic capitalism. But the traditional American value of seeking to "better oneself" is beginning to show signs of erosion. This is because it has become increasingly difficult to realize.

For most of our history, the United States has far surpassed other nations in offering its citizens genuine social mobility. That is the essential meaning of the "American dream." Now, however, many other nations do better than the United States at giving their people opportunities for bettering themselves, in the sense of moving up the socioeconomic ladder.

This is a truly astonishing change in America's relative standing in the world. If it persists, it will play havoc with our unwritten social contract, which condones large inequalities only as long as everyone has a reasonable chance to compete and to win.

An America in which income inequality grows inexorably, while the opportunities to succeed through hard work and strong motivation shrink, is a nation on a sure path to decline.

Chapter Eight

Elite Forms of Groupthink

As a social scientist and an outsider, over the years I have developed what one might call *a view from the fringe*, a view that provides an alternative form of connectedness to reality.

I've discovered that the view from the fringe frees one from being a captive of groupthink. This freedom from groupthink has often proven more revealing of reality than the vantage point of insiders.

Some years ago, after I had established myself in the field of public opinion research, I accepted an invitation to a quintessential insider pow-wow: a Bilderberg Conference.

Since its start in 1954, the Bilderberg Conference has convened annually in one or the other of its eighteen member countries in Europe, Canada, or the United States. It held its first meeting at the Hotel de Bilderberg in the Netherlands—the source of its name.

The purpose of the annual conference is to gather an elite group to discuss questions of international policy "off the record." Participants agree to a code of confidentiality, and there's no media coverage—not even a list of attendees. It is no surprise that Bilderberg has often been the target of political conspiracy theories.

The conference I attended was held in the small Swiss town of Burgenstock. One hundred and thirteen invitees attended, drawn mainly from the worlds of politics, business, banking, and the military. Many were prominent leaders and influential policy makers.

Only three of us participants identified with the views, values, and frustrations of average citizens: me, the civil rights leader Vernon Jordan, and a prominent German journalist.

Each time one of the three of us talked about how the public fit into the picture, the other participants listened courteously. But it was evident that they were bored and impatient, eager to get back to "real" issues—trade negotiations, military budgets, exchange rates, interest rates, missile counts, and so on.

Two parallel conversations were taking place at the same time. The dominant conversation focused on one set of realities. We three out-of-step participants held our own side conversation on other realities. The two groups never connected with each other.

The vast majority of the participants simply assumed that the only realities worthy of engaging their attention were a matter of either power or money. They devoted very little thought to the role of the public.

They held the opinions of the general public in mild contempt. They relished anecdotes about the public's abysmal lack of knowledge. They assumed that their own experience, judgment, and knowledge entitled them to make key decisions for their societies.

They expected that, with the help of the media, knowledgeable experts like themselves should be able to persuade the public to adopt the policies they favored. They assumed that once exposed to the "right" facts and arguments, the public would naturally agree with them and make up its mind in a timely fashion.

After conducting and analyzing thousands of public opinion polls, I had come to realize that these assumptions convey an astonishingly inaccurate assessment of how the public reaches sound public judgment about important issues.

What counts above all in reaching sound public judgment is neither factual information nor elite leadership, but rather the public's own values, feelings, interests, and cognitive shortcuts. The methods that the majority of people use to determine how well a situation matches their core values would humble those devoted to leadership-led decision making.

This Bilderberg experience was an instructive example of the outsider-insider phenomenon. I suspect that the other two out-of-step participants—Vernon Jordan and the German journalist—were also outsider-insiders like myself. Jordan, a civil rights leader, was the only black participant in the group. The journalist was well known for his independence of thought. I wouldn't be surprised if he and Jordan also thought of themselves as outsiders, and that self-perception freed them from the conventional money/power framework that seemed to hold the vast majority of participants in its grip.

I certainly was not shocked to find myself representing an atypical, outsider point of view. I had had similar experiences before. But for some reason, the experience at Bilderberg dramatized for me the divide between my own hard-won personal worldview and the worldview of the vast majority of influential men and women attending the conference.

Over the years, the erosion of thinking philosophically in our culture has never stopped troubling me. And here I was at a summit meeting of elites from the leading countries of the West participating in a blatant violation of everything I associated with sound philosophical thinking.

The Bilderberg participants were engaged in organized crooked thinking. They couldn't seem to transcend their own immersion in power politics. Focusing all their energies on this one aspect of global relationships, they were driven by their own distorted, but unrecognized, frameworks. They never seemed to pause long enough to question their underlying assumptions. No strong ethical commitment made itself heard. They were indifferent to, and even contemptuous of, the mass public.

The participants were smart. They were practical. All were deeply experienced, successful leaders in their fields. But they lacked the perspective that comes from cultivating sound philosophical thinking.

Confabs like Bilderberg have an almost primitive tribal quality—good for forging its members into a cohesive group, but bad for encouraging independent thought and sound judgment.

It was a good perch for reflecting philosophically on the lack of philosophical thinking.

Chapter Nine

From Martin Heidegger to Lloyd Blankfein

When the baby boomers were young, their goal was to create a new and better civilization in which people would be able to express their individualism in the context of a more open, fairer society that places its highest values on community and on harmony with nature.

The current state of our society is a far cry from that vision.

No organization represents this violation of the ideal of stewardship more than the hugely profitable investment banking firm of Goldman Sachs, Inc. and its CEO, Lloyd Blankfein.

Before Goldman became a public corporation, it was organized as a partnership. The difference is an important one. In a partnership, the partners are personally responsible for the firm's losses as well as benefitting from its gains. This is not the case in a corporation.

When Goldman was still a partnership, Trinity Church in the Wall Street District of lower Manhattan—New York's oldest and wealthiest Episcopal church—invited me to conduct a series of dialogues among leading Wall Street executives on the subject of corporate social responsibility.

In chairing these dialogues, I came to know (and respect) some of Goldman's top echelon of partners. Among all the Wall Street representatives in the dialogues, they held the firmest conviction that their financial transactions had to be conducted within a sturdy ethical framework of stewardship.

In contrast to some of the other Wall Street dialogue participants, they correctly understood Adam Smith's seminal insight that the invisible hand of the market works to everyone's advantage when, and only when, it is guided by a human instinct that Smith called "moral sympathy." By moral sympathy, Smith meant an inborn empathy that predisposes us to do well by others as well as by our individual self-interest. It is what I mean by an ethic of stewardship.

Several years later, Goldman ceased to be a partnership and became a corporation. As partners, top-level Goldman executives had had skin in the game. If the firm lost big, or suffered damage to its reputation, so did they. But as corporate officers they weren't at risk—at least, financially—and their ethical outlook suffered.

It became impossible to square their trading practices and conflicts of interest in the early years of the Blankfein era with the ethical stance its executives had so eloquently represented in the Trinity dialogues.

In early 2010, the SEC charged Goldman with civil fraud in deceiving its clients by actively pushing them to buy deals designed to lose money. The SEC claimed that Goldman had withheld key information from the buyers about how these deals were deliberately constructed to fail.

In his congressional testimony, Blankfein vigorously defended the firm's actions. His defense rang an all-too-familiar bell. Goldman didn't *break the law, he stated, and therefore could not have done anything wrong.* The clients who bought the tainted mortgage-backed securities, he said, were not helpless and naïve widows and orphans. They were "sophisticated investors" responsible for doing their own due diligence.

The contrast between the Blankfein narrow self-justifying mind-set and that of his predecessors is harsh . . . and unforgettable. If our culture is obsessed with individuals satisfying their own needs, limited solely by considerations of legality, the society at large will inevitably degenerate into a Hobbesian struggle of each against all.

This kind of thinking goes back to the ancient Greek philosophers, especially Aristotle, who focused on the material side of life. Such is the staying power of philosophical frameworks that Aristotle's way of categorizing reality persisted throughout the full sweep of Western history, leading eventually to seventeenth-century science and the dominance of the Newtonian framework that excludes a human factor from its theories.

Instead of the physical dimension of experience highlighted in the Aristotelian and Newtonian frameworks, the German philosopher, Martin Heidegger, stressed its human psychological nature. It is no accident that we humans are most comfortable with storytelling. Human experience invariably unfolds in time and is therefore best represented in narrative form. The story of our lives is a series of answers to the question: "And then what happened?"

This is not a question that one would pose to a pile of rocks.

Heidegger's fundamental category of human experience is that of "caring." We construct our human world out of care for self, for others, for humanity. It is caring that makes us truly human. Lack of caring is a symptom of depression, often suicidal. In a profound sense, the person who lacks care lacks humanity. To cease to care is a form of nonbeing.

There are, of course, many ways of caring. When we care deeply about others, we reach out to them in what Martin Buber called the I-Thou relationship of intimate caring. But other forms of caring are institutionalized in our culture. People care about each other in communities, companies, and organizations as well as in families, friendships, and love relationships. The youth movement originally placed a high value on communal forms of caring.

Heidegger's recognition that our heritage of Greek philosophy has willed us a very distorted map of reality—useful for describing the world of objects, much less useful for understanding human experience—is an insight of extraordinary value.

It is an accident of history that an arrogant and mean-spirited person like Martin Heidegger appears to have developed a more compelling framework for understanding human experience than more congenial and sympathetic thinkers. However unappealing Heidegger may be as a person, he does have an important insight to convey. Great thinkers are not always appealing people.

I realize that I attribute to philosophical thinking a more important role in shaping our values, perceptions, and lifestyles than do most other observers. I know that many other forces are also at work. But if I am correct, philosophy does have cogent things to say about how we should live our lives—the role that Socrates assigned to philosophical reflection.

In my view, a direct link connects the insights of Heidegger, an unappealing German philosopher writing almost a century ago, to the ethical blind spot of America's most successful investment bank.

The Goldman Sachs executives of the pre-Blankfein era whom I knew from the Trinity dialogues were hardly grand statesmen of stature. They were members of the establishment, full of old-boy snobbery and privilege. But they represented an ethic of noblesse oblige and stewardship.

They cared about others as well as themselves. They cared for the well-being of the larger society that had brought them such good fortune. They cared for the city that supported them. Above all, they cared for their clients, out of an ethic of enlightened self-interest. They knew that trust and reputation were their strongest assets, and that it would be self-destructive to jeopardize those assets.

The values of noblesse oblige, stewardship, and enlightened self-interest are expressions of caring in the Heidegger sense. They transcend the self and connect the self to the larger world of people and things beyond the self.

I fervently hope that Goldman's leaders will find their way back to their older tradition of caring for the larger community as well as for their own

narrow financial interests, that they will return to the capitalism of enlightened rather than *un*enlightened self-interest.

Chapter Ten

Transitioning to a Thoughtful Public— A Strategy

At first glance, the task of transitioning from a mistrustful, inattentive public to a thoughtful, deliberative one—shifting from raw opinion to sound judgment—might seem too formidable to undertake in today's polarized America.

But once you break the task down into its component parts, it becomes more doable. It comprises three major components—political, cognitive, and cultural—each requiring its own distinctive approach.

The political component is the most obvious one. On the political front, elites and leaders have to be willing to give the public greater say and more leverage in forging the decisions that have direct impact on people's lives.

Coming to judgment on wicked problems is hard work. You cannot expect average Americans to engage in it wholeheartedly unless they have an incentive to do so. As long as people feel their voice is not being heard, they lack the incentive to do the hard work.

I am a great respecter of what Kettering Foundation president David Mathews calls "the public voice." By the public voice, Mathews means the collective viewpoint of the American people on matters of public concern. Like me, Mathews, has come to respect the public voice, while acknowledging that it can sometimes be strident, opinionated, emotional, and dominated by wishful thinking. But as Mathews has discovered, the public voice can also be practical, pragmatic, thoughtful, generous-minded, and even wise.[1]

The strategic question is how to evoke this potential public wisdom. Our political leaders are, in principle, willing to bring the public into the decision-making process, but only under the condition that the public's input is thoughtful and constructive.

Evoking a deliberative public voice depends on the other two components, especially the cognitive one. There is a serious disconnect between what we call the public's learning curve (how the public goes about making up its mind) and our nation's methods of educating the public about issues. Decades of researching American public opinion reveal a huge flaw in how our professions, institutions, and leaders think about how the public comes to judgment on specific issues.

Our research shows that the public's Learning Curve consists of a lengthy three-stage process of absorbing and resolving difficult issues—(1) a consciousness-raising stage, (2) a "working-through" stage, and (3) a resolution stage.

The consciousness-raising stage is the shortest. The middle working-through stage is the longest because it requires people to make conflict-ridden decisions they prefer to avoid—and often succeed in avoiding for years or even decades. The resolution stage can either be long and tedious or quite short, depending on circumstances.

Our media do an excellent job in consciousness raising (stage one) but drop the ball on the other two stages. The time required for the public to go through all three stages on any one issue can take months, years, or decades (e.g., the health hazards of cigarette smoking, civil rights, gay marriage, the spread of obesity, climate change).

Ascending the public's Learning Curve usually takes longer than it should because our society lacks institutions to address the last two stages of the Learning Curve.

I have spent a big part of my long professional career interviewing my fellow Americans. That interviewing has contributed importantly to my understanding of the public's Learning Curve. In coming chapters, we will dig much more deeply into its nature and how to serve it better.

Taking into account the role of culture—the third component in creating a thoughtful public—calls for its own distinctive strategy.

The main purpose of any culture is to guide people toward what really counts. When a culture ceases to perform this indispensable function, then something must substitute for it. This present era is not a good time to depend on our culture to guide our life choices because at the moment it is too damaged to do the job.

Here is where an individual philosophy for living enters the picture. My premise is that if more Americans were to adopt a robust philosophy for living, this would at least partly compensate for our serious cultural defect.

In sum, a sound strategy for transitioning from an inattentive, erratic public to a thoughtful, deliberative public would start by revealing how our institutions might be brought into better alignment with the public's Learning

Curve and simultaneously make the case for Americans adopting a philoso-phy for living that gives priority to communal concerns.

Once these components are in place, it should not be difficult to motivate leaders to seek greater public input. Doing so will benefit them politically as well as substantively.

II

Understanding the Public's "Learning Curve"

Chapter Eleven

An Accidental Profession

Over a period of years, my work made me aware of the distinctive nature of the public's Learning Curve. Recapping how this came about is a useful way of revealing its complex nature and the many obstacles that stand in the way of incorporating it into the day-to-day practice of our democracy.

I am one of the surviving veterans of World War II. Three years of military service in the army intervened between my college freshman and sophomore years.

When I returned after the war, I decided to major in philosophy. But in my junior and senior years, I came to feel that Harvard had abandoned the magnificent body of philosophical thought that had so impressed me as a freshman before entering military service.

I therefore decided against an academic career in philosophy but resolved to continue to pursue my quest for a personal philosophy of life, whatever my eventual career turned out to be.

In graduate school, where I studied psychology, a part-time job pointed me toward my future career. One of my psychology professors had been invited by the MIT administration to conduct a study of MIT's students who were returning vets like myself. The administration was concerned because so many of their former soldier-students were having difficulty in adapting to civilian life at MIT. Their problems ranged from poor grades to suicides, with lots of dropouts and nervous breakdowns.

The university asked my professor to recommend any actions MIT might take to reduce the tensions on these students. The professor included me in his research team, partly because I had shared experiences with the MIT vets.

And indeed, I found it easy to interview (and to empathize with) disgruntled MIT returning-vet students. All of them bridled at university rules that they characterized as written for adolescents. Loneliness, isolation, and lack of direction were their constant themes. Their path seemed strewn with un-necessary obstacles.

To their credit, the MIT leadership were responsive to our findings and took immediate action. MIT discarded their outmoded parietal rules for the vets, dropped other *in loco parentis* constraints, hired a member of our team as a counselor, and instituted dances and other social events.

I found the work we had done, and MIT's response to it, admirable. Our team had applied professional skills to a troublesome problem. Our student interviews proved a great resource: the student voice conveyed a clear message. It identified a flaw in the system, which permitted us to tease out implications for remedial action. The institution responded promptly and constructively—no defensiveness, no denial, no cover-your-ass resistance.

This was my first encounter in the world of work with "stewardship." Stewardship, in my view, is an example of that thing of beauty: philosophy in action.

Shortly after this experience, I decamped for Paris on an extended leave of absence to attend the Sorbonne. Toward the end of my three-year Paris stay, and of my GI Bill money, I managed to land a part-time interviewing assignment for the Economic Cooperation Administration (ECA)—the operating unit of the Marshall Plan.

At the time, the European labor movement was largely communist dominated. The Marshall Plan's foreign policy experts wanted to sound out some of the noncommunist labor leaders.

My assignment was to do what French diplomats refer to as *tater le terrain*—getting a feel for the situation on the ground. It was a low-cost, low-risk decision to rent a freelancer to do some interviewing for them.

I developed great respect for the qualities of the men I interviewed (they were all men). They were struggling to improve the economic security of their members under difficult odds, often fighting their governments, their members' employers, and the communist labor unions all at the same time.

Once I was back in the States, I settled in New York and went on job interviews several times a week, though I didn't have a clear idea what kind of job I was looking for.

I figured that my best chance of finding the right kind of job was to offer my services as an analyst of how institutions might make themselves more responsive to the needs, wants, and expectations of those they serve—the government in response to voters, colleges in response to students, newspapers in response to readers, unions in response to their members, companies in response to employees and customers.

Today, this concept is a familiar one; in the early 1950s, its description mostly elicited a blank stare. But it did provide some guidance and unity for my job search.

To my amazement, in my second month of job interviewing, a small, offbeat firm of architects and designers offered me a job that conformed roughly to the job concept I had been describing to all willing listeners.

The name of the firm was Nowland & Schladermundt.

I liked Roger Nowland (who interviewed me) right away. He was an unpretentious engineer without small talk, highly intelligent, and unfailingly courteous. He explained that he and his partners knew very little about the consumers who used the products they designed.

He said that for the firm's male engineers, a refrigerator was merely a repository for beer and ice cubes surrounded by lots of space. They were not responsive to consumer needs.

So, he said, he had invented a concept he called "predesign research." Instead of designing products for consumers whose needs were unknown, he had the revolutionary idea of asking actual and potential users about their use patterns and needs for the products the firm was currently designing.

He had hired several market research professionals. But when they reported their results to him, they told him everything except what he really needed to know.

They reported on the age, income, gender, geography, and other traditional demographic differences among consumers. But they didn't convey any useful information about how people actually used the products the firm designed.

The market researchers were doing what they had been *trained* to do, not what Nowland hoped they would do. (They were displaying what the futurologist Hermann Kahn called "a trained incapacity" and what the French refer to as a *deformation professionelle*.)

Nowland asked me what I would do if his firm were invited to design a new station wagon for Ford, one of the firm's clients.

I answered that I had no experience either with station wagons or market research, but that I had driven a jeep in the army. I spoke about the questions I would ask myself and other potential jeep owners if someone were designing a jeep for us.

My answers appeared to satisfy him—especially, I think, my ignorance of traditional market research.

"When can you come to work?" he asked.

As I began my job, I soon realized that serving as a bridge between the people who bought and used the products and the people who designed them was no simple matter. People often *don't know* what design features in a product will work best for them.

Instead, they get used to a particular product design and adapt *themselves* to *it*, just as I was now adapting myself to working on a high stool at an architect's drawing table.

I found the work absorbing and gave it my full effort.

The interviewing techniques I had learned in my graduate psychology training and at my jobs at MIT and the ECA in Europe turned out to be useful in bridging the gap between the firm's designers and the users of the products they designed. The work of my three-person unit within the firm soon became a profit center, and eventually grew into the firm's main money maker.

There were moments of drama. One of my first assignments was a project for the Burroughs Adding Machine Company in Detroit, the leading manufacturer of quality adding machines.

To assist them in their future product planning, we conducted several hundred interviews with users of adding machines, with an oversampling of banks, their major customers. I wrote up the findings of our interviews and gave the draft to Roger Nowland, suggesting that he mail it to the company in Detroit.

When he read the draft, he called me into his office and said that I was causing what little remained of his hair to turn even whiter than it was. I became a bit defensive, assuming that he thought my findings were wrong.

My draft reported that Burroughs had fallen into a trap. Their major customers were banks, and their salespeople had contacts almost exclusively with banks rather than other types of adding machine users.

Banks require a high level of accuracy, best achieved with the full keyboard adding machines in which Burroughs excelled. However, many *non-*bank buyers preferred the ease, speed, and convenience of the simpler ten-key adding machines that Burroughs disdained to make. Another segment of the market simply wanted the lowest-priced adding machine that could do the job, a product that Burroughs also disdained to make.

The result: the company's thirty models of adding machines appealed to about one-third of the potential market, ignoring the desires of the other two-thirds.

Nowland said to me, "If I've got this right, you are saying that this fine, successful company in the adding machine business for over one hundred years is selling its products to only about a third of the market even though it has over thirty different models that customers can choose from."

I said enthusiastically. "Yes. Don't you think that's a terrific discovery! What a great opportunity for them to expand their market."

Roger said, "And you want to send the report to them by mail rather than present it in person?"

"Yes," I said. "They can read as well as we can."

He responded sarcastically, "And *you* studied psychology? You want to tell people who have been in the business for over one hundred years that they have their heads stuck up their collective asses, and you want to do it by *mail*?"

I was dumbstruck and embarrassed. I had so compartmentalized my thinking that while I was immensely gratified that our research presented the company with such a great opportunity, I hadn't given a moment's thought to the human side of the equation, the side that I eventually learned trumped all others.

Roger had me rewrite the report along more diplomatic lines. The following week, he and I took the overnight sleeper train to Detroit and in the morning presented the findings as tactfully as we could (not easy to do when the findings themselves were so brazenly clear).

When we finished, the twenty or so executives sat in stunned silence. Finally, the president said "Roger, why don't you and your assistant [meaning me] wait outside while we discuss your very interesting report?"

About an hour and a half later we were called back into the board room and asked a number of hostile questions, which we answered as best we could. We were then politely thanked and sent on our way back to New York.

On the return train, I was despondent, but Roger was quite cheerful. "Well," he said, "you've learned something, haven't you?"

I acknowledged that I had indeed learned something.

Reading the anxiety in my voice, Roger said. "Not to worry. This is going to turn out just right!"

And indeed it did. The company cut its line of full keyboard adding machines in half and introduced a new line of ten-key machines, some quite low priced. Eventually, it won a far larger share of the adding machine market.

In later years I realized how rich in philosophical lessons these early work experiences were. My part-time jobs interviewing MIT returning vets and European labor leaders had taught me the importance of an ethic of stewardship.

I also learned a lot about how widespread crooked thinking is in our society. One of my first—and most vivid—lessons in crooked thinking actually took place in graduate school. As a psychology PhD candidate, I was serving an unpaid internship at McLean Hospital, a highly regarded mental hospital close to Harvard.

In our training sessions, a staff psychiatrist would conduct an interview with a patient, and then after the patient left, he (the psychiatrists were all male) would "perform" his diagnosis. That is, he would spin a marvelously intricate story about the patient and his or her prognosis, almost always gloom-ridden and hopeless. The presentation was full of nuances and complexities. The psychiatrist would note and label as "self-evident" psychological issues that were opaque to the rest of us.

Often the performance was dazzling—with one major drawback: anytime a new *fact* about the patient emerged, it tore apart the fragile web the psychiatrist had spun so expertly.

These virtuoso performances taught me to mistrust clever interpretations of people's lives and problems that were short on facts and long on web-weaving skills.

The more general philosophical lesson I learned was how easy it was for people who specialize to lose sight of the whole picture because they are so absorbed in their specialized part of it.

Bringing a broad, synoptic overview to experience is an essential feature of thinking philosophically. Yet, the great success of science and technology is leading our society in the opposite direction—toward thinking narrowly as specialists.

The crooked thinking is not due to obtuseness; many of those making the worst mistakes are intelligent, highly motivated professionals. The problem is an extraordinary lack of philosophical thinking in our society about the limits and trade-offs of specialization, often (as in the case of the Burroughs Adding Machine Company) exacerbated by groupthink.

The lesson I was to learn over and over again was that our institutions and elites are badly out of sync with the public's Learning Curve. Indeed, they aren't even aware that it exists. And they often are not motivated to learn about it.

Doctors, lawyers, business executives, media professionals, scientists, academics, engineers, even politicians are all immersed in their own conversations and their own agendas. They develop their own language, technologies, and frameworks. Rarely do they reach out to discover how average Americans really think about issues, and how they come to judgment.

It took me many years—and an immense amount of effort—to cut through the noise and arrive at a better understanding of the distorted relationship between the public's Learning Curve and the thought patterns of elites in positions of influence.

After a few years, the novelty of the work at Nowland wore off.

I was determined not to abandon my goal of doing serious philosophical work, albeit outside a university setting. But I saw no clear path to doing so, while working full time to support my family.

One night at dinner, I was listening to the complaints of the father of one of my friends. I liked Mr. Broadwin despite the generational difference. He too was an amateur philosopher. During the day, he ran a wholesale lumber business, and at night and on weekends, he read philosophy books. We often discussed what he was reading.

That night, Broadwin was complaining about a problem with his business. Several days earlier, he had received a shipment of four hundred flush doors that were slightly faulty and therefore worthless because builders would not accept them.

I asked him if I could buy two of the doors to use as a couch and a table, provided they could be fitted with wrought iron legs. Broadwin said he would give me the doors and charge me only for the legs.

The following Saturday he arrived with the doors and the legs and together we attached them. I felt a sense of accomplishment. For a piddling amount of money, my wife and I had furnished ourselves with the base for a couch and a table I could use as a desk.

Suppose, I thought, I offered to buy Broadwin's entire shipment of the four hundred doors with their slight imperfections, opened a store in Greenwich Village, and sold them. If they sold well, we could also sell the wrought iron legs, foam rubber mattresses, and other objects that young families needed to make desks, couches, beds, and tables. I guessed they would sell quickly and profitably.

Suppose I started this new business on the side, built it up, and then sold it and with the proceeds bought myself time to do philosophy.

The more I thought about the idea the better I liked it.

The following weekend, I located a small vacant store on a side street in New York's Greenwich Village. I was able to rent it for a month (the minimum time the landlord would permit). I had the doors delivered and took out an ad in the *Village Voice* offering my inventory of slightly wounded flush doors for $9.95 each. I also had a sign painted and put in the window calling the store "Furniture-In-Parts."

The store opened the following Saturday morning and by mid-afternoon was completely sold out.

I now faced a number of practical problems. I lacked the time to do all the things that needed to be done if Furniture-In-Parts was to grow as a business. I asked Roger Nowland to reduce my hours at the design firm for a number of months so that I could launch the new business. He reluctantly agreed to do so for a proportionate cut in salary.

Several friends agreed to help out on weekends. One of my Paris buddies, Dick Dale, had returned from Paris several months prior to the opening of Furniture-In-Parts and was unemployed. He was overjoyed with the prospect of trying something new.

It was Dick who met the most daunting challenge to the store's success. Almost everyone who bought a door had some special need that required customizing his or her order. Three out of four potential customers left without buying a door because we were unable to meet their special needs. Every would-be buyer wanted their door cut down to a smaller size.

If the store were to be successful, it would have to meet these special needs. We could not hope to maintain a steady flow of business without accommodating peoples' real space constraints. (Most Greenwich Village apartments were cramped.) This requirement seemed so daunting that I was stumped on how to meet it.

Dick was unflappable. He said, "The store has a basement. We can set up our equipment in the basement; cut the doors to size; apply a strip to seal the end; bend, weld, and paint the wrought iron legs to order; and charge a few bucks extra."

It was he who later suggested that we change the name of the store from Furniture-In-Parts to The Door Store.

Several years later one of my Harvard friends opened and managed a Door Store in Harvard Square. Other Door Stores opened in other cities. The Door Stores are now a well-established national chain that has flourished since their improbable launching in Greenwich Village, more than a half-century ago.

Once The Door Store began to flourish, I returned full time to my job at Nowland and Company.

Chapter Twelve

Starting My Own Firm

I began to consider setting up my own marketing research firm.

I knew it was a risky thing to do. At the time, the economy was in recession, the unemployment rate was high, and the costs that companies usually chose to cut first were for outside services such as the one I was thinking about starting.

Moreover, I was hardly in a promising position to start a new business. As a Nowland employee, I did not have an independent reputation in the market research field. I was unknown outside the small circle of the firm's clients, and it would have been unethical for me to try to woo them away from Nowland.

But the potential benefits outweighed the risks.

With my own firm, I would be freer to seek out a different kind of research. I could look for projects that illuminate how our society's ethos and culture work—an important aspect of philosophy. I was particularly eager to write a book.

It occurred to me that my colleagues in my new firm might rebel in the event that I took big chunks of time off to write a philosophy book. They might mutiny and look for ways to get rid of me on the perfectly sensible grounds that I could not write a serious book and grow the business at the same time.

So I decided to give the new firm my own name. I would call it Daniel Yankelovich, Inc., on the premise that doing so would make it exceedingly difficult for others to replace me against my will.

My main hesitation was that the name "Yankelovich" is so awkward, ethnic, and unpronounceable, it might prove a serious business handicap. I consulted a number of knowledgeable people who all were agreed that my name on the door would constitute a serious business disadvantage. Some of them said, "If you call the company by your own name, you may get some clients in New York City, but you won't get any conservative Midwestern clients."

Their concerns struck me as reasonable, but I decided to take the risk. I had a powerful desire to make a fresh start. There is an exhilarating sense of adventure in starting anew that always excites me. I knew the risk was high, but I was confident of success.

I knew I would be bringing distinctive skills and methods that had proven productive at Nowland. They would be even more productive if I were free to follow policies I knew were sound.

I was confident that I didn't need a lot of capital. Clients traditionally paid for a third of their contracts in advance. My initial expenses would be extremely modest—a salary for me and a secretary and rent for a small office. If I had just one client, I could sustain myself for the six to twelve months I would need to find additional clients (even if they were only New York companies) to put the new firm on a sound footing.

As I thought about how to find a client, I remembered a former Nowland client, the Swiss Watch Federation, whose members included most of the prominent Swiss watch manufacturers. In my frequent trips to Switzerland on their behalf while working at Nowland, I had formed a number of personal relationships with their members, some of whom spoke only French. (My three years in Paris proved to have some practical value.)

At the time of my Nowland work with the Swiss watch executives, they had invited me to do some personal consulting. I had told them that I was unable to accept their consulting because I was a Nowland employee. They responded that their invitation was an open one and that if I were ever free to accept it, I should call them.

I decided to do so now, though with some trepidation. I had learned that people say that sort of polite thing without really meaning it. But it turned out that they did mean it. In addition, they said that they liked the idea of being my first client because they knew they would get special attention.

And they volunteered to pay in advance. Volunteered! The Swiss!

I regarded their response as a harbinger of good fortune, assured them that they would indeed get special attention, promptly rented a small office on 42nd Street near Grand Central station, and hired a sign painter to paint *Daniel Yankelovich, Inc.* on the door.

Ironically, over the next two years, I failed to land a single New York company as a client. Apart from the Swiss watchmakers, most of our new clients came from the conservative Midwestern companies that the experts I had consulted were sure that a firm named Daniel Yankelovich, Inc., could never attract.

It would take me a number of years to find out why my expert friends had been so wrong. The experience reinforced for me how powerful groupthink is and how easily it can seduce us all.

Chapter Thirteen

Part Science . . .

To my immense relief, my new company gained a profitable foothold more quickly than I had anticipated. Its reputation spread rapidly. Within two years, our staff was as large as the Nowland staff when I left it.

The new firm's first few years were the busiest of my life.

The only assignments we could acquire were those that the more established firms had flunked or were reluctant to take on. We were constantly carrying out assignments that went beyond our experience, sometimes far beyond it.

At the same time, the market research field was struggling to become more "scientific," but was going about it in a bizarre fashion.

I presented a paper to the American Psychological Association in the early 1960s describing this phenomenon as "part science, part circus."

Certainly, the aspirations to become more scientific were reasonable and fit the spirit of the times. In 1957, the year before I started my firm, the Soviet Union had startled the world with its launch of its Sputnik missile. Most Americans feared that the Soviets had forged ahead of us in the space race and were gaining competitive superiority in science. In all walks of American life, from K–12 education to marketing research, the race was on to improve our scientific literacy and competence.

Though the marketing research field had existed since the start of the twentieth century, it was only after WWII that it won widespread acceptance. One of its main appeals to business was its claim to being scientific. The credibility of that claim relied on the large-scale national surveys of consumers that were the staple of that era's marketing research.

Sampling methodology is the most reliable tool in the marketing research kit. Indeed, this methodology enjoys a scientific status comparable to the methods employed in physics and chemistry.

It is ironic that the *most* scientific aspect of polling—selecting representative samples of people to interview—seems implausible, while the *least* scientific aspect (knowing what questions to ask and how to ask them) is rarely subject to doubt.

Sampling mistakes rarely caused the many failures of marketing research in that era.

The major sources of error were: asking the wrong questions, failing to ask the right ones, using misleading language in formulating questions, and misinterpreting the findings.

This happened to GE's small appliance division. The market research director confided to us that GE's engineers had invented a small water-immersible engine and had been looking for commercial applications for it. One of the engineers had come up with the idea of using the invention to build a portable garbage disposal unit.

The business executives at GE questioned whether there would be a big enough market to warrant the investment needed to launch such an unusual product. So the company decided to conduct a survey to estimate the size of the potential market—a standard market research objective. Several months later, the survey firm they hired reported the findings to them. It reported that 8 percent of families surveyed said they would be interested in buying the new appliance.

Both the research firm and GE were confident that the sampling method was accurate—the only aspect of survey quality that was questioned in those days. It projected a potential customer base of 8 percent of forty-six million households (the number of households that existed in the country in that era).

A potential national market of 3,680,000 units looked very attractive to GE. Even if it took years to reach the full potential market, the estimate of the market's size was substantial enough to justify GE ponying up the investment dollars needed to go to production, which it did.

At this point in the story, the market research manager looked at us mournfully. In the first year of production, he told us, GE sold a grand total of 144 units across the entire nation . . . and even fewer the following year. The size of the potential market came closer to one thousand units than to the *almost four million units* projected by the market research firm. GE wanted to know what happened. They asked us to review the survey and tell them what went wrong.

Our analysis revealed a pattern that would become all too familiar to us in subsequent years. The survey's sampling technique worked splendidly: the two thousand adults the firm interviewed did indeed represent a valid cross section of the American public (as revealed by answers to other questions in the survey).

The flaw consisted of a serious error of interpretation.

We were able to show GE that people's statements of intention to buy any new product in surveys had to be the *beginning point* in a long probing inquiry, not the end point.

When someone says that they are interested in buying a product that doesn't yet exist, what they really mean is that yes, indeed, they would consider it and might even buy it *"if"*—*if* the price was right, *if* they had extra money to spend, *if* nothing else met the need better . . . *if* . . . *if* . . . *if*.

The art of estimating the potential market for a new product depends on the skill with which the various "ifs" are unearthed, probed, and tested.

Market research's love affair with scientific standards had blinded it to several realities. One was that a single tool—sampling methodology—does not by itself constitute a holistic strategy, however scientific that one tool may be.

The main flaw was a misfit between marketing research's major tool—the sample survey (polling)—and the public's Learning Curve. Surveys happen to be a good method for *quantifying* attitudes discovered through other means. But they are a clumsy, inefficient, and sometimes self-defeating substitute for interviewing people to generate insights about how the public goes about making up its mind.

Surveys provide a sound snapshot of the public's thinking at a single moment in time. But they do not reveal whether that moment falls in stage one, two, or three of the Learning Curve—an all-important fact for policy makers seeking to influence the public.

It doesn't help matters when experts in statistical methods who know little about practical marketing issues or the public's psychology conduct the surveys.[1]

Chapter Fourteen

Part Circus . . .

One of my favorite examples of the survey-linked mishaps of that era relates to the Dickensian-named Griesedick brewery of Detroit, Michigan (pronounced *greasy dick*).

One of Griesedick's family founders, a top-level executive of the company, was a member of a posh Detroit country club. He was dismayed that other members never seemed to order Griesedick beer at the club. When he asked them why they preferred other beers, they laughed uncomfortably and complained that Griesedick had a bitter taste.

The executive decided to conduct a survey to find out whether beer drinkers in the community at large felt the same way. The survey reported that, indeed, many beer drinkers did think that Griesedick was a bitter-tasting beer.

Seeking to expand its customer base, the company decided to change the taste of its beer. Shortly thereafter, the brewery's advertising blared out the news that Griesedick beer no longer had a bitter taste.

The debacle that followed almost wiped out the hundred-year-old brewery. Griesedick won precious few new customers but lost more than half of its old ones. It teetered on the edge of bankruptcy.

As with the example of the GE portable waste disposal unit, the consumer survey could not be faulted on technical grounds. Its findings were accurate: many beer drinkers did think that Griesedick had a bitter taste.

A little probing would have revealed that Griesedick's dominant image was that of a working-class, heavy-beer-drinker brew. It wouldn't have mattered to the majority of middle-class beer drinkers if Griesedick tasted like the nectar of the gods; they still would have refused to drink it.

On the other hand, for Griesedick's loyal customers—the 20 percent of heavy beer drinkers who accounted for 80 percent of the brewery's sales volume—the bitter taste was the beer's main appeal.

The company barely managed to survive, and did so only when it shifted back to its traditional bitter taste formula, gradually wooing some of its old customers back to the fold.

It never fully recovered from its marketing misstep. (Lest readers assume that only small parochial companies are prey to this sort of mistake, the Coca-Cola Company—a model of marketing sophistication—made a very similar sort of blunder with its New Coke.)

Yet another common mistake in the use of consumer surveys related to shaping advertising messages. Many companies conducted surveys to find advertising themes that would convince consumers to buy their brand. But when they applied the survey findings too literally, they sometimes unwittingly gave consumers a reason *not to buy* their product.

The Dow Chemical Company, for example, did a survey to learn how best to advertise its then new plastic wrap, Saran Wrap. The survey showed that heavy users of Saran Wrap liked three features of the product: its transparency, its self-clinging characteristics, and its ability to protect the food wrapped in it. Applying the survey findings literally, the company advertised all three features, with equal emphasis on each.

The most important benefit of Saran Wrap is, of course, its ability to protect food. That is what justifies the higher price of the product. Though the company's advertising did mention this benefit, it didn't come across to potential buyers as cogently as the product's transparency. Consumers were comparing it to wax paper; that was what they were used to using.

What they got from the advertising was the message that "Saran Wrap is a transparent wax paper"—a benefit that surely didn't justify a higher price.

Saran Wrap sales didn't improve until the company stopped advertising its transparency and instead focused exclusively on its ability to protect the food wrapped in it.

I like these kinds of examples because they illustrate the complexity of everyday life even in the relatively simple domain of marketing products.

Most market researchers of that era assumed that technical proficiency in survey sampling, interviewing, and statistical analysis would automatically produce useful results without requiring them to understand the marketing problems they were addressing.

I have come to think of this blind spot as "technological hubris"—a naïve overconfidence in the power of technical methods to solve complex human problems. This is just one variant of the all-pervasive groupthink that dominates our society.

Repeated failures on the part of market surveys made them vulnerable to competition. A variety of professionals from other disciplines rushed in to fill the vacuum, creating a circuslike atmosphere of "send in the clowns."

Alfred Politz was the leading practitioner of conventional market research surveys in that era. The Politz practice of conducting surveys with cross-section samples of one thousand to two thousand consumers was the most popular market research method of the 1950s and early 1960s.

Politz's nemesis was the motivation research guru, Dr. Ernst Dichter. Dichter was trained in psychoanalysis. He derided the "superficiality" of statistical surveys that, in his view, gave "a false patina of science" to marketing research.

Instead of "nose-counting" surveys of thousands of people, Dichter typically conducted just a few dozen so-called depth interviews to which he brought a strict Freudian interpretation, usually sexual in nature. He called his method "motivation research."

It was the motivation research craze that brought a circus-like atmosphere to the market research field of that era. Dichter's interpretations were like a high-wire act without a safety net.

When Ford introduced a car with radically changed style lines, the new model featured a sloping front end in contrast to the squarish Ford look of preceding years. Sales fell almost immediately and Ford used motivation research to find out why. The motivation research interpretation was that Ford's male buyers did not want to buy a "castrated car."

This interpretation was not only unhelpful to Ford from the point of view of practical action, but it ran smack up against the spectacular success of Volkswagen, whose lines sloped even more dramatically than Ford's. The motivation research interpretation of the failure of Ford's ill-fated Edsel model was that its front end looked too much like a vagina. Ford's mistake with the Edsel was far more serious than faulty design: in seeking to compete with General Motors, it had built a car for a market niche that no longer existed.

Motivation research informed us that we chew gum because we are a nation of frustrated breast feeders. It told us that the effects of early toilet training explained our reactions to toothpaste. It explained that we experience canned soup as warm and nutritious as mother's milk, and that our liking for soup carries us back to the uterus, arousing "prenatal sensations of being surrounded by the amniotic fluid in our mother's womb."[1]

When a woman baked a cake, motivation research told us that she was symbolically re-creating the process of giving birth. Using a cigarette lighter, it explained, expressed a "desire for mastery and power . . . the need for certainty that a lighter will work . . . is bound up with the idea of sexual potency."[2]

Everywhere one looked at that time, motivation researchers were applying to consumer brand-choice decisions concepts developed from psychopathology—the professional study of the crippling, sometimes tragic conflicts of human life.

Such trivialization is not just bad tactics; it is also bad taste and vulgar manipulation. Small wonder that the advertising and marketing of this "Mad Men" era were regarded with suspicion and mistrust.

The conflicting frameworks of Politz and Dichter were just one more example of the common philosophical failure to keep the whole in view at all times.

Politz's surveys pushed the method of sampling beyond its limits, producing reams of impressive statistics that were technically accurate but often useless, and sometimes downright misleading. Dichter felt free to generalize wildly from a handful of depth interviews to millions of people.

Consequently, the market research field was ablaze with doctrinaire arguments pitting Politz versus Dichter and surveys against depth interviews. It was a ridiculous debate, akin to arguing about whether a hammer was better than a saw, without reference to whether you wanted to drive in a nail or cut a board.

Since the two methods were erroneously assumed to perform the same function, they were treated as competitive rather than complementary. Rarely were they combined in the same research project. The market research field seemed blind to the reality that the two tools had radically different capabilities. The Dichter method was useful for making observations and generating hypotheses; the Politz method was good for measuring the level of generality of the observations and testing hypotheses.

At the time, I was so busy getting my new company off the ground that I gave little thought to the reasons for our ready acceptance in the marketplace. In retrospect, I think the reasons are unmysterious. We benefitted from the circuslike appeals of the competition. We must have sounded like the voice of common sense.

We spoke plain language rather than psychobabble or statistical correlations. We honed in on the clients' problems and addressed *their* anxieties, not our own. We used a variety of research tools, each one suited to its own specialized use, rather than applying the same method indiscriminately to all problems. One of my new firm's areas of specialization was conducting probing interviews where intention to purchase became the jumping-off point for a long inquiry, rather than its end point.

We focused on results, not methodology. And we produced solid, actionable findings that made sense to our clients.

To my great surprise, my background in psychology and philosophy had proven far more relevant—and practical—than I had ever imagined. I was uniquely well prepared to cope with the near chaos in the marketing research field.

My graduate school training in Freudian psychology, for example, gave me a huge advantage in assessing the claims of motivation research. Again and again, I was able to detect the psychological bullshit that threatened to swamp the field.

One of my new firm's clients, the Coty perfume company, had hired a motivation research firm to help them communicate the special appeal of their leading perfume. The motivation research pros immediately honed in on sex. They said that the company's perfume was seen as having a strong sexually seductive appeal, and that its advertising should feature this theme.

But when we interviewed a cross section of Coty perfume users, we found a quite different consumer psychology at work. Coty's scent was perceived as light, floral, and expensively elegant. For these users, the Coty perfume served first and foremost as the finishing touch on those occasions when they wanted to complete their most "dressed-up" look.

Their association with the Coty scent was with formal social occasions when they wanted to look their best. As one of them remarked, "It was like wearing a very fresh, dainty pair of white gloves."

In this case, the relevant psychological themes related to femininity, self-enhancement, and social acceptance. These are familiar and often relevant themes in consumer psychology. Why schlep in heavy-breathing sexual connotations when they are neither relevant nor useful?

Sometime later, I had the opportunity to read the interviews that the motivation research people had conducted. They were, in fact, well done. Quite professional in their execution, they were full of useful information, and strongly confirmatory of *our* interpretation.

The motivation research experts who had initially analyzed them were so committed to sexual interpretations that they read what they wanted to read into the interviews. Their own preconceptions, not the content of their interviews, had dictated their interpretations.

The state of soul in which one contends with life's deepest problems is of a different order than that involved in choosing a brand of beer or fragrance of perfume. Consumer psychology involves relatively trivial decisions. Conflating the trivial and the existential constitutes the worst sort of thinking and judgment.

Chapter Fifteen

Smart People, Dumb Mistakes

We have always lived with dumb people making dumb mistakes. But now we are inundated with very smart people making very dumb mistakes.

One of the most important social research projects of the times—the so-called Midtown Project—is a good example of how specialization caused smart researchers to lose sight of the whole, and thereby undermine the purpose of their research.

The Midtown Project was an ambitious and promising study of mental health, whose formal title was "Mental Health in the Metropolis."[1] Its stated purpose was to gain a better understanding of how the urban environment affects people's mental health.

The project's centerpiece was a survey conducted among New York City residents ages twenty to fifty-nine, randomly selected from a total population of 110,000 adults living in a heavily populated neighborhood of Manhattan. All 1,660 respondents participated in detailed two-hour interviews. Two psychiatrists reviewed all the interviews, treating each one as if it were an individual case history.

It took the researchers *eight years* to plan, conduct, analyze, and publish the results.

I was enthusiastic about the study because of its scale and rigor. It promised to yield insights into the impact on people's mental health of living in a densely populated urban environment, as well as solid documentation of those influences. I could hardly wait for the results to be published.

But when they were, I was disappointed and troubled. I couldn't understand why the findings were so stale and simplistic. As I reread the methods section of the study, I quickly understood why I felt so let down.

In stating the rationale for their methodology, the authors wrote, "The interpersonal environment refers to a universe of enormous proportions and

67

complexity." Therefore, they continued, instead of the "sightless groping" that would be required to "search the environment for clues and leads to conditions associated with mental illness," they would instead "select . . . a few theoretically promising (and technically researchable) landmarks for exploration."[2]

I laughed out loud. These "technically researchable" landmarks turned out to be the same old demographics—age, income, education, socioeconomic status, ethnicity, and religion—that had so frustrated Roger Nowland because of their lack of relevance to his market research projects.

The senior psychiatrists participating in the study were well aware that many urban environmental influences affect mental health—the stresses of city life, insufficient loving attention to child rearing, erratic discipline, the influences of gang and drug culture, time pressures, parental abandonment, the presence of addiction, and other dysfunctions.

But these factors were way out of the comfort zone of the specialists who carried out the survey. They fell back on socioeconomic status and other familiar forms of demography.

In relying almost exclusively on demography and ignoring the myriad other urban influences, the researchers abandoned any realistic hope of identifying and documenting what they claimed they were looking for; namely, the *most important* urban influences on mental health.

A phenomenon like mental health is complex, elusive, mysterious. The whole point of the research was to scan the full range of urban influences in order to discover the strategically most important ones *from the point of view of action and intervention.*

You cannot gauge the relative importance of forces if you exclude them from investigation.

The social science landscape is too vast to be covered by a single science or discipline, hence the need to carve it into manageable pieces. But the carving calls for exquisite thought and care, which it has never received. Instead, the thought and care is concentrated *within* each area of specialization, with very little devoted to figuring out how to put them together to solve complex problems.

Very little thought and care is devoted to figuring out how to establish or to cross those borders, but a great deal goes into enforcing them.

I have been conducting marketing and social science research for more than a half century and *never once in more than fifty years* have I encountered a single important problem that fell clearly within the boundaries of any one of the isolated social science disciplines. Not once!

Economics is the perfect example. Economists pay exquisite attention to their own central concepts such as supply and demand, but up to quite recently have been naïve when it comes to assumptions about people's actual economic behavior.

In his testimony before Congress in 2008 to explain the causes of the credit crisis that had brought the American economy to its knees, economist Alan Greenspan, the once revered head of the Federal Reserve, confessed that he was shocked to realize that mindless groupthink and frenzied lust for short-term profits had almost destroyed the American banking system. The subprime mortgage crisis had caught him totally by surprise!

Economist Paul Krugman believes the majority of American economists missed the great recession of 2008/2009 because they were seduced by *the wrong philosophical framework*. He describes how economists fell in love with "the idealized vision of an economy in which rational individuals interact in perfect markets . . . gussied up with fancy equations."[3] Blinded by their philosophical dogmas, the nation's leading economists insisted that the nation's housing markets were essentially sound at the very moment that they were falling off the cliff.

This blind spot among economists has nothing to do with their empirical observations of how markets actually work (the presumed basis of economic science). It has everything to do with groupthink—the tendency of people who belong to the same profession or group to latch onto a particular way of thinking, however misguided it may appear to outsiders.

Groupthink can occur at many different levels, from the micro-level of the family and the intimate social group to the macro-level of entire civilizations. Certain industries and institutions, such as the Wall Street financial community and the automotive industry (when it was concentrated in Detroit), have shown themselves especially prone to groupthink.

Every field of thought has its own groupthink framework—its network of assumptions and core beliefs. These are almost never made explicit, and indeed the group itself often is not conscious of its own framework.

The underlying framework of economics, for example, presupposes that the economy is a self-sustaining, self-correcting, largely autonomous entity. This has distorted our picture of how most economies function. In actuality, economies are not autonomous or isolated from the rest of society. They are deeply embedded in the norms and politics of the larger culture.

In recent years, a new branch of economics has come into existence, called "behavioral economics." It focuses on how people actually behave, not on how economists theorize they should behave.

This is a welcome development. But it should have been unnecessary. The insights that economists need about people's economic behavior under various conditions exist in abundance in related social sciences and marketing research. We now have a new generation of economists reinventing the wheel and doing amateurishly what other social sciences do professionally.

The other social sciences also huddle, each on its own isolated island, occasionally venturing into bridge-building projects that the purists in their field regard with contempt. The shortsighted groupthink among the nation's bankers that Chairman Greenspan swallowed whole would not have surprised any competent sociologist or psychologist. On the other hand *they* would not have taken the trouble to understand the workings of the banking and investment systems.

I have come to think of the artificial boundaries dividing the social sciences from one another as a major methodological mistake. I think of it as "the fallacy of false borders."

In my new firm, we asked ourselves: is there any way to transcend the false boundaries that isolate psychology, economics, sociology, political science, psychiatry, and marketing research from one another, in the interest of solving our clients' problems?

In today's society, specialization is the mother of most dumb mistakes made by smart people. It could hardly be otherwise. If you insist on looking at only one aspect of any complex issue, you are bound to be misled and to mislead others.

The sort of straight thinking that philosophy insists upon is not an arcane academic skill; it is a practical necessity for solving serious problems.

Chapter Sixteen

New Methods of Conducting Research

Over a period of years our firm introduced a handful of useful innovations in the methods for conducting market and social research, most of them related directly or indirectly to the public's Learning Curve.

One of these innovations is a form of interviewing in which people are encouraged to talk as volubly as possible about the *meaning* for them of certain objects and experiences, depending on the subject of the research.

I called this method "phenomenological interviewing" because it is based on the principles of the school of philosophy known as "phenomenology." The purpose of a phenomenological interview is to elicit the fullest possible range of meanings, associations, and values that objects and experiences have for people.

The experience might be deep and profound (what it meant to be brought up in Nazi Germany as a Jew), or it might be superficial (choosing one scent of perfume over another).

I have used phenomenological interviews in many research projects to gain a better understanding of what it meant to

- oppose or support the wars in Vietnam, Iraq, and Afghanistan;
- hold a strong ethnic identity;
- grow old;
- vote for one particular presidential candidate;
- give up smoking cigarettes;
- be addicted to drugs or drink;
- live in a housing project;
- try to break out of poverty;
- put one's own expressive needs ahead of sacrifice for the family;
- buy a small car rather than a large one;

- be relocated from one city or home to another; or
- experience the 9/11 terrorism and other hinge moments in American life.

The advantage of this type of interview is that you don't have to *infer* what experiences mean for people. You can reveal their full network of meanings empirically by probing each meaning for its linkages to other webs of meanings. This technique has proven to be a boon for data-based research.

Another innovation was to integrate qualitative and quantitative research methods into a single unified research strategy.

I had an enlightening experience with the comparative strengths of these two methods when I was in Harvard's graduate program of clinical psychology. The main research tool used in those days was the qualitative case history, a variation of the depth interview.

Controversy over the causes of schizophrenia had been the subject of heated discussion in our classes. I reviewed the case histories of young schizophrenics whose chances to live a normal life seemed nearly hopeless. At first I was unable to discern any consistent pattern that would cause so devastating an outcome for patients.

And then I came upon a research report based on a sample survey of *hundreds* of schizophrenics.

An underlying pattern nearly leapt off the pages of the report. Cognitive malfunction—the lack of the ability to think logically and stay connected to reality—was much more prevalent than emotional turmoil.

This pattern suggested that brain malfunction might be the root of the disease, rather than a psychosocial cause such as sexual or emotional abuse.

In the survey of schizophrenics, none of the patients was analyzed in the depth and detail that the individual case history permitted. On the other hand, the common characteristics of the mental disorder stood out far more clearly in the large survey of schizophrenics.

This encounter proved a Eureka moment for me. I learned that integrating *both* methods—case histories *and* sample surveys—was far superior to total reliance on one method or the other. It made me realize that qualitative and quantitative methods can serve different purposes and are best used in tandem.

A particularly poignant hypothesis revealed itself when our firm was hired to conduct phenomenological interviews with urban women living in Columbia Point, a public housing project located in an isolated area of Boston mired in poverty and terrorized by violence. The purpose of our interviews was to look for possible strategies of intervention—ways to help these women escape from the miseries of being trapped in Columbia Point.

Most of the project's residents were single mothers, struggling to cope with life in the project against formidable odds. Our interviews invited the women to describe what living in the Columbia Point Project meant to them, and also what it might mean to them if and when they were able to leave it.

Analyzing the interviews, we were struck by a sharp difference in outlook that divided the women into two groups—those who expressed some degree of control over their lives and those who felt more fatalistic. (They lacked any sense of efficacy or control—what psychologists refer to as a "sense of agency.") Life was something that just "happened" to them. They automatically assumed that they had nothing to say about it.

Our government client had assumed that the women would need just a little help to help themselves. But the research strongly suggested that while interventions that depended on self-help might assist women with a normal sense of agency (typical of middle-class populations), they would be futile for women whose self-conception did not include a sense of agency. For these women a far different mode of intervention would be required.

In other words, our interviews suggested that at least for this goal in this urban population, the most relevant variable was a psychological trait (a strong or weak sense of agency) that easily could be measured in a survey through just a few questions. From a methodological point of view, the interviews gave rise to a hypothesis that could readily be tested either experimentally and/or in a survey.

I had this experience in mind when I found myself disappointed with the results of the Midtown Project. Had the Midtown Project researchers used phenomenological interviewing with a small selection of their subjects prior to conducting their large sample survey, they would have uncovered many links between the stresses of city life and the subject's feelings of agency, self-esteem, well-being, and other mental health issues. These insights could have led to a strategic focus on the most important urban mental health influences and enormously enhanced the survey's practical value.

The most helpful feature of the phenomenological interview is that it can generate hypotheses. Its serious limitation is that you cannot reliably use it to generalize to the population at large.

Surveys have the opposite strengths and weaknesses. Their great strength is that they *can* measure how representative (and even how intensely) feelings and attitudes are distributed among large populations—provided you know *what to measure and how to measure it*. Their most serious limitation is that they are not very productive in generating hypotheses.

For the past forty years, my research with large populations has combined qualitative methods—phenomenological interviews, focus groups, and case histories—with quantitative surveys. The population might consist of consumers, voters, the general public, corporate employees, college students, judges, investors, scientists, business executives, or mental patients. The qualitative methods reveal how people think and make up their minds; the quantitative methods measure how representative are various attitudes and opinions about the subject.

   In each case, our firm's innovation was to demonstrate that the integration of *qualitative* and *quantitative* methods yields the most revealing and reliable insights.

Chapter Seventeen

Research Designed for Action

All of our firm's innovations came about in our search *for the best way to solve a specific problem*, rather than seeking to understand it better. This makes a huge difference in how you design your research.

Oddly enough, in the academic world of the social sciences, research designed to *understand* a problem is often held in higher regard than research to *solve* the problem.

This has always seemed perversely wrong-headed to me because it is based on the false assumption that *understanding* a problem is the key to solving it. This is not true for the toughest problems, the "wicked" ones, the ones that should be irresistible to high-powered university research departments.

It is possible, for instance, to *understand* the causes of childhood obesity or why our education system fails so many children from a poverty background or why action on climate change encounters so much resistance or why many of our cultural norms are dysfunctional, without having a clue about how best to *intervene* to solve these problems.

Also, our firm specialized in how large populations of people, as distinct from individuals, think and behave. Differentiating between the two is not a familiar distinction, but it is an important one.

Population behavior can take many forms, for example, crowd behavior, mob behavior, market behavior, and subculture behavior. All have distinctive characteristics. Since population behavior has not been studied as thoroughly as individual behavior, there is lots of room for new insights and innovations.

Our most original and important innovation was discovering *the decisive mode of segmentation* for solving problems involving large populations of people.

Among the myriad ways one can differentiate among groups of people, the key question is often this: What is the *one most useful way* to subdivide groups of people to achieve your objective—reduce obesity, increase savings for retirement, motivate people to do something about the dangers of climate change, and so on?

If you want to discourage people from using their cell phones while driving, what interventions will work with what segments of the driver population? If you want to encourage young people in poverty populations to stay in school and achieve higher educational credentials, what is the best way to segment that population to discover ways to do so? If you want to improve people's mental health, what forms of intervention are best suited for what forms of mental distress?

In making this judgment, the most important consideration is *actionability*, not understanding.

A number of years ago, I reviewed three surveys that studied people's cigarette-smoking habits. The sponsor of one was a cigarette company whose interest was to *encourage* smoking. The sponsor of the second study was the American Cancer Society whose interest was to *discourage* smoking. The sponsor of the third was a university research effort to understand the *differences* between smokers and nonsmokers.

All of the studies were technically proficient. All three used traditional academic methodology. All revealed a wide range of differences between smokers and nonsmokers. But none of the three studies revealed strategies for intervention—either to *encourage* or *discourage* smoking—because they had neglected to discover the decisive mode of segmenting the population from the point of view of action.

Americans stopped smoking only when lawsuits revealed that cigarette companies had been lying to them about the health hazards of smoking.

Many ways of dividing populations are revealing, intriguing, amusing, or statistically significant. But most of them don't tell you much about the most practical way to intervene in order to produce real change.

Our firm developed the methodology of the decisive mode of segmentation in our consumer research work. While consumers differ from each other in many ways, there is usually one particular difference that is decisive for shaping marketing strategy for a particular product. The key to strategic success is to discover that one *best* way from among *all* the ways consumers differ from one another—demographically, attitudes, felt needs, values, meanings, feelings, habits, brand loyalty, susceptibility to messaging, to name a few.

We used this innovative technique with our firm's very first client: the Swiss Watch Federation, the ones who had trusted me with their reputation and with enough money to go into business.

Its members were all of the famous brands of Swiss watches, and almost all were in trouble. They were hoping that the research techniques I had developed could help them dig themselves out of it.

Back in the mid-1950s, the Swiss watch industry had begun to worry about sharp increases in the U.S. sales of Finnish-manufactured Timex. They commissioned a survey from their American ad agency to confirm their assumption that the low-priced Timex appealed primarily to low-income consumers. The survey showed that, indeed, low-income buyers were purchasing Timex. But it also showed that higher-income people were also buying Timex watches.

This finding troubled and confused the Swiss watchmakers. The ad agency's survey did not reveal the reasons for Timex's breadth of appeal, nor did it point to any remedial course of action. Its major finding ran counter to the blind-sided assumption of the Swiss watchmakers that the only reason anyone would prefer a Timex over a Swiss watch was because they couldn't afford the superior Swiss product.

So the Swiss industry did what it was always comfortable doing: it watched fretfully without taking any serious countermeasures. As it watched, Timex continued to gain market share, quarter after quarter, year after year.

Timex sales grew inexorably until it became the *largest-selling watch in the world*. The company's growth, from virtually zero to the world's best-selling watch, is one of the most dramatic success stories in marketing history. Timex not only ate the Swiss industry's lunch, but their breakfast, dinner, and chocolate snacks as well.

The first thing our new firm did when the Swiss Watch Federation invited us to research the watch market was to conduct some phenomenological interviews to get a better grasp of the meanings that watches held for their owners and how they influenced their buying behavior. The interviews revealed a wide range of meanings.

Some watch owners assigned a strong *sentimental* meaning to their watches. Their watch symbolized an emotional attachment to a family heirloom or to a gift given on a special occasion.

For others, possessing a fine Rolex or Patek Phillipe or Omega watch (all Swiss) meant *status and prestige*.

Other watch owners valued the elegance of their watch as a *fine piece of jewelry*.

For many watch owners, their timepiece embodied fine functional quality. They assigned a high value to the *workmanship* of any watch that wouldn't lose more than a few minutes of time a year.

For some consumers, quality also meant that their watch would *last indefinitely* without requiring them to replace it for decades.

Yet other consumers simply wanted a *cheap watch to tell the time* without fretting about its quality or precision, and were quite willing to replace it when it broke down—if it was cheap enough.

Having identified some fifteen to twenty different meanings associated with owning a watch, we then had to decide which ones to quantify in a follow-up survey. The purpose of the survey would be to help us plan marketing strategy for the Swiss watch industry. To do so it was important that the survey focus on the most strategically promising ways of addressing the key segments of the watch market.

Our phenomenological interviews had revealed that the buyer's income was not the key to watch marketing strategy. Many upper-income consumers were buying Timex watches instead of highly precise Swiss watches because a watch held no special emotional meaning for them beyond telling the time. These are people who want to pay the lowest possible price for any watch that works reasonably well.

This was not this group's attitude toward all products, just toward watches. The same people who bought a cheap Timex might buy the most expensive TV set or automobile because these products had special meaning for them. They just didn't assign any special value to their watches.

With this information, we segmented the watch market into three groups:

Segment One: people for whom a watch means nothing more than a way of keeping track of time;

Segment Two: people who value their watch's *functional* quality (e.g., precision of time keeping, quality of workmanship, reliability, and durability); and

Segment Three: people for whom a watch holds both functional *and* emotional value (e.g., as a gift, as jewelry, as a status symbol).

Focusing on this mode of segmentation, the survey that followed was quite revealing. It showed that approximately one out of four watch buyers (23 percent) fell into the first segment—those who wanted to pay the lowest possible price for a watch and who were willing to throw it away and replace it at any time.

The largest segment—almost half of all watch buyers (46 percent)—fell into the second segment. These were the consumers who respected product quality and were willing to pay extra for it. They valued watches for their long life, good workmanship, and styling but had no sentimental attachment to their watch.

The third segment, 31 percent of watch buyers, valued a watch both for its emotional meaning and its product quality. For many of these people, their watch symbolized a special occasion—a graduation gift, a job promotion, an important anniversary. Fine styling, a quality brand name, or a gold or diamond case enhanced the emotional value of the watch.

Our segmentation analysis clearly showed that all of the Swiss watch companies were concentrating their product design, pricing, distribution, and advertising on *this 31 percent segment*. They virtually ignored the other two segments—69 percent of the market.

The advertising implications of our segmentation analysis were particularly striking. Most watch brand names at the time, companies like Longines, Bulova, Hamilton, and Omega, were linked to the Swiss watch industry. Hamilton advertised its watches as a gift of love—appropriate for Segment Three but not for the others. Longines and Omega stressed the prestige of their brands—again appropriate mainly to Segment Three. They advertised in higher-income Segment Three media like the *New Yorker* magazine, neglecting TV and other media aimed at the mass market.

Bulova, however, focused on Segment Two buyers. It hammered away at the slogan, "See the Bulova difference," pointing to Bulova's waterproof and shock-resistant features. Bulova had spent many millions of dollars and years of effort to equate watch quality with being waterproof and shock-resistant.

Cunningly, Timex built its own sales on Bulova advertising. Its ads stressed the fact that consumers could buy waterproof and shock-resistant Timex watches for $14.95 instead of Bulova watches at $79.95. People in the first two segments flocked to Timex.

In sum, the survey demonstrated to the Swiss that they were unwittingly ignoring more than two-thirds of American watch buyers.

The Swiss sold their watches almost exclusively through jewelers, while the majority of watch buyers bought their watches in other kinds of retail outlets such as department stores and drug stores. Also, the Swiss advertised mostly at Christmas time, while the majority of consumers bought their watches year round. As a result, Timex had the bulk of the market virtually all to itself, while the Swiss clung to the illusion that they were competing effectively.

Our research demonstrated that the Swiss watch companies did not have *the right line of products, the right styling, the right pricing, the right distribution, or the right advertising* to meet the requirements of 69 percent of the market. They lacked the most elementary market strategy.

The president of the Swiss Watch Federation at that time, Mr. Vallat, who was also president of the Omega Watch Company, was so gratified by the research that after I finished my presentation in Bienne, Switzerland, he impulsively snatched his gold Omega watch off his wrist and pressed it into my hands. He was acting generously in true Segment Three fashion, presenting me with an expensive personal gift to mark a special occasion.

I have Mr. Vallat's valued gift in my top drawer. It still works splendidly more than forty years later. I cherish it, but I don't wear it. I wear today's

Japanese equivalent of the Timex, a $19.95 watch, which I am obliged to replace frequently because of its cheap wristband. (The watch itself keeps on working.) I too am acting according to the script: the Segment One part of it.

In developing the decisive mode of segmentation, we refused to *assume in advance* that the best way to segment populations would always be demographic. At first glance, this might seem a mere technical step. But it gradually became clear to me that both in marketing and social research, it called for judgment and substantive knowledge.

Most marketing problems such as the Swiss watch problem are far simpler than societal problems, say, in reforming health care, adopting sound energy policies, acting effectively on climate change, improving K–12 education and social mobility, offering affordable higher education to more people, and enhancing the ethical aspects of our market economy. Marketing problems tend not to be wicked. Social problems are almost always wicked.

The two fields require radically different research strategies. On social issues, it is almost impossible to test any one factor in isolation from its larger cultural context. You can't solve policy problems unless you can cut through all of the noise, confusion, and complexity of this context by finding the one strategy that leads most directly to effective intervention.

Chapter Eighteen

Never Present More than One Idea at a Time

Once I realized that the decisive mode of segmentation was such a useful analytic tool, I was eager to share it with others.

Encouraged by the results of the Swiss watch experience, I accumulated a number of other examples of research projects that exemplified the decisive mode of segmentation in action. When I had a total of ten, I drafted an article to document the concept (with the uninspired title "New Criteria for Market Segmentation") and submitted it to the *Harvard Business Review*. To my great satisfaction, the *Review* accepted the article and published it about six years after my firm was founded.

Following its publication, the *Review* received large numbers of requests for reprints of the article. Forty years later in 2004, they invited me to revisit the subject and to write a follow-up article discussing the fate of the segmentation ideas and concepts I had proposed in the earlier piece.

In the later piece, "Rediscovering Market Segmentation" (written with a colleague, David Meer), I tried my best to be tactful; but frankly I was horrified by how badly the original idea had been distorted. [1]

In the 1964 article, I had emphasized the dangers of confusing *segmentation* with *typologies* of personality. The three profiles of watch buyers we had discovered in our segmentation analysis emphatically did not represent three types of personalities—cheapskates, compulsive timekeepers, and sentimentalists. They represented something far narrower and of greater interest to watch companies—profiles of values and meanings *specific to watches and only to watches*.

In the 1964 article, I wrote,

> We are not dealing with different *types of people* but with differences in people's *values*. A woman who buys a refrigerator because it is the cheapest available may want to buy the most expensive towels. A man who pays extra for his beer may own a cheap watch. . . . By segmenting markets on the basis of the values, purposes, needs and attitudes relevant to the product being studied we avoid misleading information derived from attempts to divide people into types.[2]

I realize that the temptation to divide people into types is almost irresistible. Jung categorized people into introverts and extroverts. David Reisman divided the population into inner-directed and other-directed types. Most of the time, developing typologies is a harmless enough sport.

In advertising circles, the sport is known as *psychographics*—profiling people by differences in their psychological as distinct from their demographic characteristics (e.g., traditionalists vs. risk takers; planners vs. impulse buyers; hedonists vs. puritanical types). This way of profiling people is intuitively satisfying because we almost always recognize someone we know who fits the typology.

Relying on typologies in marketing is almost always useless. Indeed, it may give you misleading information about the fundamentals of marketing: planning a product line, pricing, finding the right kinds of retail outlets, developing new product features, and designing products to fit each market segment. Even in advertising, its value is limited to helping the advertiser achieve some degree of initial rapport with the consumer.

This critical distinction between segments and typologies was largely ignored by the market research community, especially among advertising agencies who fell in love with profiling people by types of personalities.

In the 1980s, psychographic profiling became a powerful fashion in marketing, thanks largely to the work of the Stanford Research Institute. In 1978, Arnold Mitchell and his colleagues at the Institute launched VALS—an acronym for their Values and Lifestyles Research Program.

VALS classified the entire American population into eight psychological types derived from peoples' responses to a large-scale VALS survey, drawing on the theoretical frameworks of sociologist David Reisman and psychologist Abraham Maslow.

The VALS types include

innovators,
thinkers,
achievers,
experiencers,
believers,
strivers,
makers, and

survivors.

These VALS typologies may have added to our pool of knowledge. They surely added to the pop psychology literature. They reflected the typical academic approach to applied research: you develop a theoretical framework and apply it wherever it seems plausible to do so, without any genuine attempt to understand its strategic importance in relation to the problem it purports to solve.

The dismal consequences are hardly surprising. As we reported in our 2004 *Harvard Business Review* article, only 14 percent of two hundred business executives stated that their companies had derived any real value from the segmentation studies they had conducted.

Demographic or psychographic profiling may suggest a variety of ways to tackle a problem. But they won't reveal the *one best way*. Finding the best solution for diverse populations depends on discovering the decisive mode of segmenting the population *for the purpose at hand*.

This was my first, but not my last, experience with how difficult it is to make an idea clear to others.

In retrospect, I realize that I had asked for trouble in my 1964 article by attempting to convey two ideas at the same time. I broadened ways to profile consumers so as to include values, meanings, and behavior as well as demography.

But I *also* proposed adding a step to the survey research process in order to find the one most decisive mode of profiling the consumers of any specific product. Big mistake.

Happily for me and for the firm, the decisive mode of segmentation had proven its value by the time we found ourselves in the role of recognizing and monitoring the cultural revolution that began in the sixties and seventies.

Chapter Nineteen

Tracking the Cultural Revolution

In the spring of 1965, I was invited to meet with an executive named Blake Newton—the CEO of the Institute of Life Insurance. I expected a buttoned-up bureaucrat and was agreeably surprised to be greeted instead by a gracious, relaxed, and entertaining Virginian who in tone and manner reminded me of other gracious Southerners in my life.

His concern was that mystifying changes taking place in our culture might constitute a threat to the life insurance business, and he wanted to know whether the social sciences could either confirm his fears or put them to rest.

The life insurance industry, he said, was founded on Protestant ethic values of self-sacrifice, hard work, postponed gratification, and living for the future. He had begun to wonder whether the goings-on in our nation's leading universities, such as Berkeley, might be a harbinger of changes that could undermine the Protestant ethic values that had for so long dominated mainstream American culture.

He invited me to review the social science research literature to test his hunch that our nation's young people were gravitating away from the traditional values that supported the life insurance industry.

I told him I would love to do so, and I truly meant it. When, several months later, I reported my findings to the annual meeting of the institute, Blake Newton's hunch proved prescient. There were early warning signs of a shift away from the traditional values of hard work, self-sacrifice, and post-ponement of gratification.

But at that time, the shift was confined to a minority of the nation's college students. Most eighteen- to twenty-five-year-olds, including the majority of college students, shared their parents' traditional values and outlook on life.

Like their parents, they were satisfied with their lives, their work, and their opportunities to get ahead. Mainstream America, including the vast bulk of its youth, endorsed our nation's traditional Protestant ethic values with enthusiasm and conviction.

However, a minority of college students had adopted a more contrarian stance. I shared with the insurance executives my conviction that this minority could well prove to be a "forerunner group"—a precursor of things to come. Virtually all of the students in this group came from affluent families. Though their numbers were small, I said they were likely to swell in the future as affluence spread and as the nation's youth cohort doubled in size.

At that time, Lyndon Johnson's War on Poverty was focusing public attention on the poorest, least educated segment of Americans. But in my report to the institute, I warned:

> We should not overlook the crisis brewing at the other end—among the small number of college students from affluent families who have already achieved (or know that there lies readily within their grasp) the benefits of education and material well-being for which the majority of young people strive. [1]

Leading social scientists of the day, such as David Reisman, had developed their own theories about the nature of this group's gripe with mainstream American values.

The young males in this forerunner group typically spurned conventional corporate careers as being boring and meaningless. Reisman theorized that these careers were scanting the nurturing needs of these young men. In his words, they seemed to be in pursuit of "familism rather than careerism" and were more interested in "building nests than fortunes." [2]

My research suggested that the young women in the college forerunner group had a different quarrel with our traditional values. They rejected a life built exclusively around domesticity but were uncertain about how they could balance domestic life and a career outside the home.

Both the young men and women in this forerunner group were restless, anxious, full of doubts about society and its values (though not about themselves and their own values). They were quite vocal in letting the world know how dissatisfied they were.

The report intrigued the life insurance executives. Blake Newton won their support for our firm to conduct an annual study of changing American values. We called the tracking study MAP—an acronym for Monitoring the Attitudes of the Public.

A number of social movements were stirring things up. The civil rights movement challenged our racial values and attitudes. Ralph Nader's consumer movement questioned the safety of American automobiles and other products. The anti–Vietnam War movement stirred up so much political conflict that it brought down the Johnson administration. The women's movement was beginning to gather momentum.

Of all of these, the one movement that would eventually prove to have the greatest impact on the nation's cultural values was the *youth movement*, led by the forerunner sons and daughters of America's increasingly affluent middle class.

I found it ironic that the businessman Blake Newton had intuitively grasped the nature of this new youth movement faster and more accurately than had leading social scientists.

For many generations, our traditional value structure, though complex in its details, had been remarkably simple in overall design. The vital force urging it forward had been *socioeconomic mobility*, the main engine of self-improvement.

Achieving respectability, economic security, and middle-class status had persisted through the postwar years as the primary motivating forces in American life. This triple goal is what the vast majority of young people meant by "improving their lot in life." This was the goal that most Americans were willing to sacrifice for.

But it was a goal the forerunners were beginning to challenge. The young men and women in the forerunner group were beginning to ask questions such as

"What must we sacrifice to achieve more affluence and social status?"
"Is it worth it?"
"Are such sacrifices even *necessary* in a time of rising affluence?"

These privileged college students had the luxury to raise these questions because, unlike the vast majority of Americans, their families had already achieved considerable affluence and social mobility.

In the 1970s, following the lead of the student forerunners of the 1960s, a majority of Americans would raise these same questions. The trends we identified marked the beginning of the most momentous transformation in the American ethos since the Civil War.

Until Blake Newton came along I hadn't realized the extent to which a major industry—life insurance—had so thoroughly grounded itself on the same cultural values that shaped individual norms. Newton's fully justified fear was that as Americans stopped sacrificing for the future, their motivation for buying life insurance would be undermined.

I had pretty much swallowed the economists' conception of business as a pure economic phenomenon, following the laws of supply and demand and profit maximization. In reality, many businesses are thoroughly embedded in the larger culture, though usually not to the same extent as life insurance.

I began to see the many social movements of the times in a new light. Previously, I had assumed that it was exclusively political and economic injustices that gave rise to social movements. This was true of the leftist social movements of the Great Depression, and it was also true of the civil rights movement.

But most of the social movements of the sixties originated from other forces.

Shoddy and unsafe cars inspired Ralph Nader's consumer movement. Frustration and the thwarted potential of women drove Betty Friedan to write *The Feminine Mystique*, launching the women's movement. The shocking title of Rachel Carson's book *Silent Spring* launched the environmental movement. The youth movement was grounded in the self-fulfillment hopes of privileged youth.

None of these movements was led from the top. All were spontaneous, bottom-up phenomena. They provided a glimpse of what can happen when the great beast of culture bestirs itself. The results are not the same as the kind of unrest that political and economic inequality inspires.

In college I had had some exposure to the discipline of anthropology and the importance it attached to culture. But in tracking the 1960s cultural revolution, I came to appreciate the immense transformative power of culture to shape our values and ethos, and how unstable that power can be. And I was thrilled with our opportunity to study such a revolution.

Once Blake Newton had opened the door for us, I was determined to keep it open.

Chapter Twenty

A Special Brand of Rebellion

I had stuck my neck out by labeling a segment of college students as "forerunners," implying that their attitudes and values were likely to predict future trends. I had also stated that, contrary to the prevailing view, *political* radicalism was not the major thrust of the students' concerns (though the majority fiercely opposed the war in Vietnam).

It was certainly obvious that the Vietnam War and the draft lottery were exercising an enormous influence on forerunner student attitudes. But I suspected that these antiwar attitudes were masking a deeper and more enduring change in our culture.

Without fresh measurements, however, there was no way to document what was happening beneath the surface.

It took me several years of scrounging to find clients willing and able to provide the funding for further research. Finally, two of the nation's major media outlets—*Fortune* magazine and CBS News—came through. The *Fortune* breakthrough came first and was the key to inciting the interest of CBS News.

In late 1968, *Fortune* commissioned our firm, Daniel Yankelovich, Inc., to conduct a national study among college students and young adults who didn't attend college. We were to test my hypothesis that a college-based forerunner group held bold new attitudes and values that were likely to spread to the larger culture, including the majority of young Americans who were not in college.

Fortune assigned the project to one of its top editors, Daniel Seligman, and published the findings of our survey in a two-part article written by Seligman in January 1969 under the title, "A Special Kind of Rebellion."

The article stated,

The different attitudes registered between those who had and those who had
not attended college are clear-cut—but not very surprising. What is perhaps
most surprising in the data is the sharp division within the college group.

The sharpest divide in the college student population was the motivation
for going to college. The main motivation of the majority of students (58
percent) was the practical one of earning more money, pursuing a more
interesting career, and achieving a better position in society.

But a large minority of college students stated that they took these practical benefits for granted and were, therefore, unconcerned with them. Most of
these students came from affluent families and majored in the arts, humanities, and social sciences rather than in business or engineering. For them,
college meant something far more intangible than social and economic mobility.

It was this second group that we labeled "forerunners."

In his article, Seligman observed that answers to the survey questions
were

remarkable on two counts: first, for the extraordinary rejection of traditional
American values by the forerunner minority, and second, for the similarities in
the beliefs of the majority of college students and those who have not been to
college. On many questions these two groups are closer to each other than
either is to the forerunners. [1]

Our research showed that in the late 1960s, nine out of ten Americans
ages eighteen to twenty-five continued to embrace traditional American values and attitudes. This 90 percent majority comprised noncollege youth plus
the practical-minded majority of college students.

The forerunners represented about 40 percent of college students—a paltry 1 percent of all Americans!

As of October 1968 when we conducted the *Fortune* survey, the values
and attitudes of the forerunner group turned out to be an odd stew of various
ingredients. It was the first documentation the nation had of the size and
nature of this phenomenon, the cultural revolution.

Its advocates voiced

- condemnation of our culture as a "sick society,"
- yearnings for greater opportunities for self-expression and greater toler-
  ance of individual differences,
- greater freedom to "do your own thing,"
- an idealistic determination to transform American society, and
- rejection of the war in Vietnam.

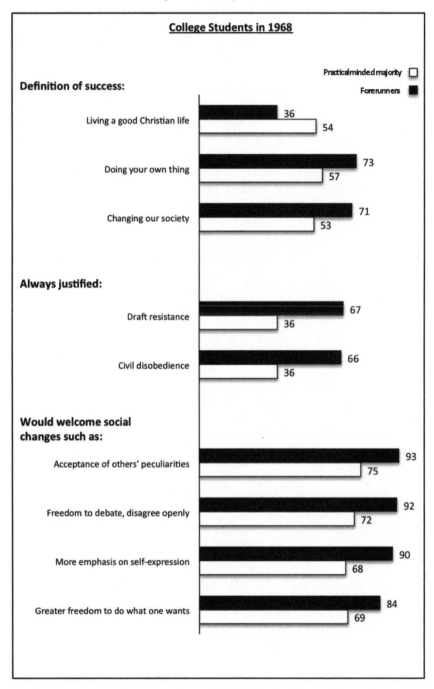

Figure 20.1. College Student Differences in Values. Original data presented in Daniel Seligman's "A Special Kind of Rebellion" *Fortune* (January 1969).

One feature of this now ancient *Fortune* study has enduring significance: the sharp divide among college students of their motivation for attending college. At that time, almost six out of ten said their reasons for attending college were the practical ones of earning more money and finding better jobs ("the earners"). About four out of ten held more intangible, less practical motivations ("the learners").

"Earners" now form a much larger majority, for the simple reason that the era of high-paid/low-skill jobs is long dead. College has become a precondition for earning middle-class incomes.

I suspect that online education as it evolves may tear our current higher education system apart. It is unlikely that both types of motivations can be satisfied by offering a four-consecutive-year residential experience. The difference between earners and learners reflects the sharp social class and cultural divisions in our society.

In the future, I believe, the practical-minded majority will gravitate toward institutions that feature online instruction and real-life apprenticeship, leaving the traditional residential experience to the more elite-minded minority.

Chapter Twenty-One

Who's Afraid of the "Generation Gap"?

In the late 1960s, two interpretations of campus-based unrest dominated the news. One was that a huge generation gap had opened up between America's youth and older generations. The other was that our youth had become radicalized under the influence of the New Left and the war in Vietnam.

In 1969, CBS News decided to do a three-part series of one-hour specials to explore these two interpretations under the heading "Generations Apart." Because of our work for *Fortune*, our firm was invited to conduct the research for the shows.

CBS wanted to gauge the depth and extent of the generation gap in general, and in particular to assess how politically radical American youth had become. The network permitted us to interview not only college and noncollege youth, but also a cross section of their parents.

The TV series aired in May and June of 1969. CBS published the detailed findings of our survey in a pamphlet titled "A Study of the Generation Gap Conducted for CBS News by Daniel Yankelovich, Inc."[1]

The overall conclusion of the CBS report was that "the large majority of youth . . . retain traditional American values." The so-called generation gap was pretty much confined to a small minority of American youth, concentrated among America's most affluent, best-educated young people.

The media loved writing about the generation gap and our politically radicalized youth. But the business community found these phenomena deeply disturbing. Our nation's business leaders feared that it was not blue-collar workers who might foment a revolution but rather the most affluent class of Americans—indeed in many instances, their own sons and daughters.

My research had convinced me that the generation gap theory was a misleading cliché, and that the "radical" politics of forerunner college youth masked an even more fundamental shift in social values. I was sure that the radical politics of most college students was directly tied to the draft lottery and the war in Vietnam and that it would dissipate whenever they did.

The dominant telephone company at the time, AT&T, invited me to write a series of articles for their journal *Bell* on whether or not the "revolution in values incubating on the nation's campuses posed a critical challenge to business."

The articles for *Bell* gave me the chance to surmise what might be going on beneath the surface of the political turmoil of the times, and to unravel what I suspected was the early stage of a transformation of traditional American culture.

Here are some quotes taken from these *Bell* articles. They sum up what I thought at the time (1969) was really going on in our youth culture.

> The New Values, as I shall call them, are highly correlated with several generations of college education that, in our society, usually means several generations of material comfort as well.
>
> These New Values are still in a formative stage but certain themes emerge clearly among forerunner students. The young forerunners warmly embrace technology as a means for achieving humanistic goals. They are also busy working out new conceptions of religion, sexual morality, and patriotism, seeking to purge our older love-of-country of its nationalistic pride and will-to-power—luxuries they feel humankind can ill-afford in an atomic age.
>
> As long as the war in Vietnam continues, these differences in perspective will remain sharply polarized. But once the war is settled, the true nature of the New Values will emerge more clearly, divested of their ideological overtones. For the New Values antedate the war in Vietnam. They had been incubating at least since the 1950s. [2]

Here is an echo of the distinction that philosopher Hannah Arendt makes between liberation and freedom. Liberation is freedom *from* unwelcome conditions; freedom is freedom *to* achieve some positive goal.

The forerunner college students were concerned with both liberation *and* freedom.

In private life, they sought liberation *from* the stultifying social conformity of the 1950s, especially with respect to sex and what they saw as a corrupt "money chase."

In public life, they sought liberation from the most nationalistic forms of patriotism and prejudice. But over and above liberation from constraints, they also sought freedom—not just for themselves as individuals, but also the freedom to enhance public life in the larger community and improve its responsiveness to the will of average citizens.

In the seven tumultuous years from 1967 to 1974, I managed to find funding for six national studies of America's youth—an average of almost one a year. One of the studies focused exclusively on changing values of college youth; five of them covered both college students and the noncollege majority of America's young people.

The JDR 3rd Fund (named for John D. Rockefeller III) took the leadership role among private foundations in providing funding and persuading other foundations to chip in. John D. himself took a keen interest in the research and personally helped to raise money from other foundations for some of the studies.

Rockefeller personified the so-called "establishment" of the era—the elite individuals who exercised an outsized influence on the direction of our society. Many of their college-age sons and daughters were vigorous activists in advancing the nation's cultural revolution. Their well-heeled parents were more than casually interested in their views; they were obsessed with the subject.

In those years, I presented our research findings to many managerial audiences. Because their sons and daughters were involved, their interest was intense. Every nuance of our research findings seized their fascinated attention.

Chapter Twenty-Two

High-Risk Experiments without a Net

The most startling trends of the cultural revolution are those that transformed the American family.

In the 1970s, the nation's birthrate plunged from 3.7 children per family to 1.7. The number of single households more than doubled. By the end of the 1970s, a majority of married women (51 percent) had entered the workforce, including large numbers of women with children under the age of six. Increasing numbers of women also sought higher education credentials. For the first time in our history, more women than men entered college. Simultaneously, the number of working-age men (ages sixteen to sixty-five) dropping out of the workforce nearly doubled.

The "typical American family" almost disappeared. Those households with a male wage earner, a female homemaker, and one or more kids had plunged from a solid 70 percent majority of all households to a paltry 15 percent!

In 1980, I wrote *New Rules—Searching For Self-Fulfillment in a World Turned Upside Down.* In the introduction I stated,

> What is extraordinary about the search for self-fulfillment is that it is an authentic grass-roots phenomenon involving perhaps as many as 80% of all adult Americans. It is as if tens of millions of people had decided simultaneously to conduct risky experiments in living.
>
> And the experiments *are* risky. Acting boldly in the name of self-fulfillment, many people are startled to wake up one day and find themselves with a broken marriage, a wrong-headed career change or simply a muddled state of mind about what life choices to make. . . . There is something about the times that stimulates Americans to take big risks in pursuit of new conceptions of the good life.

What was that something?

I suspected that the answer lay in America's spontaneous reassessment of the practical, "instrumental aspects" of life versus its "sacred/expressive" aspects.

"Instrumental" aspects are those not valued for themselves, but as means to an end. A tree, for example, might not valued for itself but only as a source of lumber.

From this utilitarian point of view, a person might be valued merely as a good worker or a desirable sex object or helpful in meeting some other need or desire.

In opposition to the instrumental, to be "sacred" in the sociological sense is to be valued for yourself.

In the American culture of the 1970s, the sacred/expressive aspects of life assumed greater importance for tens of millions of Americans. In *New Rules* I wrote,

> The domain of the expressive is always opposed to the instrumental. . . . Myths, art, poetry, monuments, story-telling, song, dance, customs, architecture, ritual, the harmonics of nature—all make expressive claims over and above any instrumental purpose they may serve. . . . *At the heart of the self-fulfillment search is the moral intuition that the very meaning of life resides in its sacred/expressive aspects.*[1] (emphasis added)

As Americans invested more of their attention on the sacred, they transformed the implicit but powerful "giving/getting compact—unwritten rules governing what we give in marriage, work, community and sacrifice for others, and what we expect in return."[2]

In the life histories I gathered for *New Rules*, my respondents were typically quite clear about the terms of this giving/getting compact in their own lives and how and why they wanted to change it for themselves. The culture's "unwritten rules" had become as arbitrary to them as a wild card in poker.

- A number of men and women refused to stay in moribund marriages after their children had grown.
- Many women rejected the idea of depending exclusively on their husbands' earnings when they themselves were capable of adding substantially to the family income.
- A number of women stated with amazement that it had never even occurred to them that they could choose not to have children. They said, "If you are a woman, that is what you are expected to do."
- Others told stories of how their parents had given up doing what they really wanted to do with their lives because sacrifice was expected of them.

• Many men complained that they had been obliged to stay in jobs they disliked solely because it gave them the means to provide for their families.

Average Americans set out to prove that life could be more than a series of sacrifices for others or a grim economic chore. They were "determined to give more meaning to their lives, to find fuller self-expression, and to add a touch of adventure and grace to their lives and the lives of others."[3]

By the time I wrote *New Rules*, the changes that Blake Newton had foreseen not only had occurred but had surpassed his, and my, expectations:

• The Protestant ethic of working for the future became regarded as old-fashioned. Working at a job just to make a living no longer had intrinsic value; it wasn't a sacred activity, but a means to an end. Sacrificing for others was no longer accepted as an important value: why do it if it wasn't an economic necessity?
• The concept of marriage and family changed to suit the individuals involved: rather than social norms assigning the participants traditional roles, individuals and groups developed their own ad hoc definitions.
• Women came to feel as if they had been treated instrumentally as means to a social (and masculine) end. They insisted on being treated as sacred: defining for themselves their sexual, marital, family, work, and citizen roles.
• Social customs, behavior, expectations, and demands were reconsidered as noncompulsory.
• All kinds of authority and rules were questioned or regarded with suspicion.
• Introspection, spirituality, self-expression, and the human connection to and responsibility for the natural world assumed increased, almost religious respect.

A more comprehensive inventory of the changes that swept the nation in in the first few decades of our cultural revolution is on the next page.

This inventory of changes reflects powerful forces at play: intense focus on the self and its satisfactions; the quest to replace some of the instrumental chores of life with more of its sacred/expressive aspects; determination to change the terms of the traditional giving/getting compact; willingness of Americans to take risks with their lives, sometimes recklessly.

Looking back, I was far too optimistic about the positive forces at play in the society. I thought that the narcissism and self-centeredness of the era would eventually give way to a new ethic of commitment, stewardship, and community.

I underestimated the power and appeal of unrestrained egoism—the imperatives to put one's own needs and desires ahead of all other values.

DAILY LIFE—FAMILY AND WORK:

Marriage roles. The ideal of shared responsibilities replaces obligations based on rigid husband/wife roles.

Family. Americans continue to value family life while greatly expanding the meaning of family to encompass childless marriages and nonlegally binding relationships.

Work ethic. Work for its own sake is no longer regarded as having intrinsic moral value. Instead, Americans look to their work as a source of personal satisfaction as well as of income.

Women's rights. Women should achieve self-fulfillment by following paths of their own choice, rather than through roles dictated by society.

PUBLIC/SOCIAL BEHAVIOR:

Authenticity and rejection of hypocrisy. Greater freedom for the individual means avoiding forms of social conformity that do not truly express one's individuality. We should forgo polite, socially acceptable forms of hypocrisy and present ourselves naturally and honestly.

Less respect for authority. We should pay less heed to the authority of institutions and experts and rely more on our own capabilities to choose the mores and lifestyles that suit us best. All forms of authority are met with suspicion.

Pluralism and diversity. Differences in ethnicity and lifestyle are widely accepted and valued as a statement of one's sophistication and lack of prejudice. In all walks of life we should strive for more diversity and acceptance of differences.

Social conformity. Less value is placed on keeping up with the Joneses. The notion of conforming to the judgment of others loses its constraining force.

Respectability. Norms dictating the correct behavior for people of a particular social class are eroded, even mocked.

The concept of duty. What one owes to others as a matter of obligation no longer counts as much as it did in the past. Sacrificing one's own interests is seen as questionable moral accounting.

Sacrifice. Less value is placed on sacrifice as a moral good replaced by more pragmatic criteria of when sacrifice might be required. Rarely, sacrifice may be necessary, but only in a sacred cause.

OUR WORLD:

The environment. Greater value is assigned to respecting and preserving nature and the natural. Rather than conquering nature, emphasis is placed on cherishing and preserving the quality of land, water, air.

Social morality. Observing society's rules is no longer deemed important as long as one isn't breaking the law.

OUR BODIES, OUR SELVES:

Sexuality. Less moral value is assigned to sexual behavior. Sexual norms are considerably liberalized. The implicit contract of giving female sexual favors in return for male commitment is disregarded, as is commitment as a requirement for sexual intercourse.

Health. Awareness of the importance of maintaining and enhancing one's own health is greatly increased. Rather than assuming health or illness is beyond one's control, emphasis is on intervention to prevent problems and enhance physical well-being.

Introspection and spiritual hunger. People are expected to have deep spiritual hungers that crave expression and to reach higher levels of self-understanding.

Expressiveness. Choices of products and lifestyles express one's individuality rather than one's social status. People are encouraged to make more of their own choices and to find new ways to express their unique inner nature.

Pleasure. Pleasure, especially its bodily forms, is regarded as good. Puritanical disapproval of pleasure is rejected.

Self-enhancement. Self-enhancement means many things—not only expressing one's individuality through one's physical appearance but also cultivating one's cultural tastes through more gracious living and becoming a well-informed individual with thoughtful worldviews. Self-improvement comes to mean striving for physical, aesthetic, and intellectual growth, rather than either showing off financial success or flaunting one's moral sacrifices.

Chapter Twenty-Three

America Tells Itself a New Story

A cultural revolution is a rare event in the history of any nation or civilization, occurring only once or twice every few centuries. It took me a long time to realize that I was living in the midst of one.

The young forerunners whose enthusiasm launched the cultural revolution didn't realize the extent to which the ideas they were promoting had been distorted by extraneous influences such as the war in Vietnam, the Kennedy and Martin Luther King Jr. assassinations, the advent of birth control pills, the transient political radicalism on college campuses, their own youthful moral absolutism and rebelliousness against authority.

Before adopting the revolutionary label for these far-reaching changes, I did some research to learn how thoughtful scholars use the term *revolution* as applied to these sorts of tectonic shifts in culture.

The philosopher Hannah Arendt presented the most original and suggestive definition of revolution. For Arendt, all revolutions—cultural *and* political—introduce "a new story" in human affairs. By new story, Arendt means a new beginning, a genuine novelty in the human adventure. [1]

The task I set myself was to discover that new story.

To illustrate what she means by a new story, Arendt cites America's colonial experience decades prior to the political revolution of 1776. She insists that a *cultural* revolution preceded America's *political* revolution. It was this colonial cultural revolution that gave rise, Arendt argues, to a genuine new story in human society.

The main thread of the new story was this: *mass poverty is not inevitable.* Arendt states that throughout prior history it was automatically assumed that the great mass of people would always live out their lives in abject, and I mean *abject*, poverty. This was particularly true in seventeenth-century Europe.

But colonial America was a society with almost no poverty, as Europeans understood the term.

Colonial America thus provided the European Enlightenment with a new model of what is humanly possible. Arendt writes, "The social question [of mass poverty] began to play a revolutionary role only when in the modern age, and not before, men began to doubt that poverty is inherent in the human condition." The *new story*, then, was that "life on earth might be blessed with abundance rather than cursed by scarcity."[2]

At this point Arendt introduces a controversial—but to me wholly valid—idea. She states that genuine freedom for the individual always involves the larger community—the society and culture to which all of us belong. This is that aspect of life she says the Romans referred to as the *res publica*—the public aspects of our lives, as distinguished from purely private life. Our freedom involves having a voice in those decisions our society makes that have an impact on our own lives.

If others make those decisions for us—experts, elites, politicians, policy makers (however benign their intentions)—then, Arendt says, we may be liberated but we are not truly free. A public voice in political decisions is an indispensable aspect of freedom.

The cultural revolution of our own time may have overlooked this important insight. We may have achieved liberation, but not true freedom.

What *is* the "new story" that our current cultural revolution tells? What does it say about the two quintessential themes of American culture—the search for freedom and the hunger for greater material well-being? Has our liberation—launched in the 1960s from the constraints of the conformist 1950s—led to more freedom? Or has it undermined it?

In retrospect it is clear that the sixties and seventies did (as Blake Newton feared) undermine the values of the Protestant ethic. Its collapse revealed that these values not only had supported the life insurance industry but also formed one of the ethical pillars of our distinctive American culture.

The essential feature of the Protestant ethic, as elaborated by sociologist Max Weber, is its emphasis on *sacrifice* and *constraint*. Leisure, pleasure, and play are to be sacrificed for hard work. Personal gratification is to be postponed. Care and concern for others are to be placed ahead of self-interest. Respectability is to be achieved through conforming to the expectations and demands of others.

The appeal of all this sacrifice is the promise of highly valued but *postponed* rewards—the bettering of the self materially, socially, spiritually.

The present cultural lurch in our ethos has transformed the national psychology

- from a Depression outlook to a psychology of affluence (at least up to the Great Recession of 2007–2009);

- from a single, conformist lifestyle to a blazing, bewildering array of lifestyles;
- from a unified conception of marriage and family to a flexible range of meanings;
- from an ethic of suppressing one's sexuality to permission to express it freely;
- from a bigoted stance toward minorities to a more tolerant one;
- from a willingness to sacrifice for the greater good to an untrammeled individualism; and
- from a clear distinction between morality and legality to a blurring of the differences.

The convictions of the nation's forerunner college students in the 1960s had two main elements. The first was that affluence had made the sacrifices characteristic of the fifties lifestyle unnecessary. The other was that the most unnecessary—and undesirable—sacrifice was that of the expressive aspects of the self.

Forerunners insisted that they had the right to choose the lifestyle that suited their own individual temperament. They saw no reason to conform to the expectation that they must give up what is most precious to them in the interest of making a living and bringing up a family.

The cultural revolution also reveals some useful insights into the nature of culture.

It shows that culture can change with surprising speed.

It suggests that while lurches can take place quickly, it is not easy to put the pieces together again and adapt smoothly to the changes.

It shows that what we came to call the "lurch and learn" process can cause culture to grow dysfunctional and misleading for long periods of time.

It implies that culture cannot by itself dictate what constitutes a flourishing civilization; human nature acts as a constraint on culture. However difficult it may be to tease out the differences between nature and nurture, there are big differences and they matter a lot.

The early phase of the cultural revolution in the 1960s, while it was still confined to the college campus, emphasized the larger community as well as the individual. In its origins, it presented a vision of human flourishing that would truly constitute a new story in human affairs.

I belong to the generation of WWII vets who came of age before these transformations took place. It was our children—the baby boomers—who spearheaded the cultural revolution. I served both as astonished witness to its unfolding, and also as a tardy participant and beneficiary.

It would be unfair to criticize the entire baby boom generation for leading the country in the wrong direction. The fault lies in the turn taken by the nation's cultural revolution over the past few decades.

The always-delicate balance of tensions between self and community has tipped in favor of self. Ideologies have sprung up that rationalize the desires of the self. Ironically, a cultural revolution that began in deep appreciation of the values of community has come to betray those values. We have become what sociologist Robert Bellah calls "our insanely individualistic American society."[3]

Chapter Twenty-Four

The Yankelovich Monitor

Consumer buying habits often reveal trends in the larger culture. Our firm's marketing research was beginning to detect far-reaching changes in consumer behavior.

Few consumer products mirror social trends as faithfully as automobiles. In postwar America, our automotive industry had grown accustomed to designing their product lines to match the public's social status aspirations.

In reflecting the status hierarchy of the times, no one did a better job than General Motors, with a line of cars carefully calibrated to celebrate each step up the status ladder. Upwardly mobile consumers could signal their improved fortunes with a more expensive and prestigious make of General Motors cars. The Chevrolet brand represented the lower social status, while the Buick, Pontiac, and Oldsmobile brands each represented a step up in social status. The Cadillac brand topped the line.

Other automakers envied GM's ability to cover such a wide swath of the status hierarchy. Ford, in particular, was determined to match GM's success in covering the full range of status niches.

Ford knew its cars were competitive with GM at the two ends of the status hierarchy: at the low end, the Ford brand offset the Chevrolet; at the high end, the Lincoln brand competed successfully against the Cadillac.

But in the middle-status range, Ford had only one offering, the Mercury, pitted against GM's three entries—Buick, Pontiac, and Oldsmobile. This was Ford's main motive for introducing the ill-fated Edsel. The Edsel was targeted to increase Ford's share of market in this middle-status range.

At that time, the late 1950s, many explanations were offered for the Edsel's dramatic flop, including the suggestion that its distinctive frontal design offended our sexual sensibilities.

However, our firm's marketing research suggested a less titillating cause: namely, that consumers were growing less obsessed with cars as status symbols and more interested in cars as forms of self-expression and personal identity. Instead of your automobile conveying your social status, it would serve as a statement about what sort of person you were, or aspired to be.

At first, Ford's marketing executives rejected this interpretation, though in later years, Ford did learn to capitalize on this trend with cars like the Thunderbird.

Nor were cars the only products reflecting changing consumer values. By the late 1960s, markets began to show the influence of the consumer's new attachment to the natural. Food products, especially breakfast cereals, were obliged to feature all natural ingredients.

The trend also affected women's clothing. Clothing styles grew more casual and "natural looking." Even women's undergarments were obliged to show the same concern with nature and the natural. Indeed, the changed demands of women stunned the undergarment manufacturers. You might say, in fact, that the bottom dropped out of girdle sales, and the market for bras drooped badly.

As these marketing research experiences piled up, they convinced me our society was definitely changing.

Most of our clients seemed bewildered by the enormity of the impact of cultural change on their businesses. They were accustomed to looking at their markets mainly through a competitive lens: they expected major challenges to come from competitors in their own industry, not from external social forces.

My associate, Florence Skelly, immediately recognized the business opportunity that this change of focus represented for our firm. Since every new cultural trend affected a wide range of businesses, Florence proposed that we initiate a new business service to track the new trends and analyze their impact on a variety of products.

The same social changes affected very different types of business—for example, naturalism's influence on both breakfast cereals and bras. Thus, noncompeting clients could be kept up to date with the same information.

Clearly, this was an appealing business model to clients since they could share the costs of research with other companies. Florence's insight gave us something to offer that was truly unique and unlikely to be replicated by clients trying to keep up with cultural change on their own.

We recognized that funding the new service would require an upfront capital investment we didn't have—hundreds of thousands of dollars. Florence was convinced that the potential growth and stability the new service would bring would be well worth the investment. I knew she was right, though I didn't know how we would raise the capital.

We decided to go ahead and hope for the best.

Florence volunteered to do most of the heavy lifting in developing the new service, which we called the Yankelovich Monitor, and we made swift progress.

While we were pondering how to find the capital to launch it, a solution appeared out of nowhere. We began to receive inquiries asking whether we would be willing to sell our firm.

I was unprepared for such a radical move because I had always assumed that no one would want to buy a professional firm like ours. I had assumed that buyers were only interested in purchasing companies that made real products, like furniture or machine tools or sneakers or cameras, the sorts of products our clients made. But a new business era had come into being. Professional firms based on the services of a handful of individuals were being acquired for substantial sums of money.

As soon as I realized that Daniel Yankelovich, Inc., might be a logical target for acquisition, I loved the idea. The more I thought about it, the more problems it promised to solve. First of all, the company acquiring our firm would undoubtedly want to invest the capital needed to develop the Yankelovich Monitor, on the premise that it would greatly enhance the firm's value.

In the second place, I knew that Florence and my other partner, Arthur White, were concerned about their own financial situations. At the time, I owned 100 percent of the company. They were making major contributions to its success, and I regarded them as full partners and wanted to share ownership with them. If the firm were to be acquired, their ownership stake could mean real money for them. All three of us would benefit, which is what we all wanted.

And finally, of importance to me personally, I might achieve the kind of financial independence that would let me pursue my philosophy vocation.

Two big obstacles to selling the firm remained. One was that we cherished our independence and were horrified by the prospect of outsiders who didn't understand our business starting to micromanage it—the fate of many professional firms that had sold themselves to larger companies.

The other obstacle was financial. I had no hesitation in sharing ownership with my partners, Florence Skelly and Arthur White, but doing so meant that my share of the booty we would receive for the firm would not be enough to insure my financial independence.

Amazingly, the solution we devised to overcome these two obstacles worked exactly as we had hoped. That doesn't happen very often. We developed a buyout arrangement with the prospective new owner, a computer leasing company named Leasco.

Leasco would give us a down payment based on a multiple of our current earnings, plus enough capital to launch the Yankelovich Monitor. In turn, the three of us would agree to a five-year employment contract, enough time to develop and market the Yankelovich Monitor and rake in whatever earnings it added.

At the end of the five-year contract, Leasco would then make a second payment to us based on a multiple of the added earnings. If the Yankelovich Monitor were successful, the second payment would yield enough additional money for me to have the financial independence I had sought for so long. It all depended, of course, on the Yankelovich Monitor's becoming a success. Of that we harbored few doubts.

What made the contract irresistible to us was Leasco's contractual commitment not to interfere in the management of our business during the full five-year period when we were striving to earn the extra payout.

We knew we were taking a risk. Leasco's owner and founder was a young financier, Saul Steinberg, who had gained a reputation as a raider and financial buccaneer. We didn't know whether we could trust him to maintain the hands-off role the contract called for.

But we figured that as long as we were making progress, he would keep his part of the bargain, if for no other reason than that we were such small fry in his scheme of things: at the age of twenty-six, Saul had attempted to take over the crusty Chemical Bank of New York, a favorite of powerful financial interests. He would have succeeded if the governor of New York, Nelson Rockefeller, had not intervened on behalf of the bank.

Through Saul, I eventually got to know most of the big-time players (such as Michael Milken) in the wild financial scene of the times.

Saul scrupulously kept his word. He invited me to join his board of directors, and as an ironic result, over the five-year period of my contract, I interfered in his business more than he did in mine.

Just before signing the final papers, we changed the name of our firm from Daniel Yankelovich, Inc., to Yankelovich, Skelly and White. It was under that name that the firm achieved its greatest successes.

The Yankelovich Monitor did not disappoint.

Chapter Twenty-Five

Founding the Public Agenda

Two events in 1975 brought about my career shift from studying how consumers make up their minds to investigating how citizens do so.

The first was an invitation from *New York Times* editor Abe Rosenthal to help *The New York Times* develop its own proprietary public opinion poll. Rosenthal knew about our firm's work through several projects we had conducted among employees of *The New York Times* when its writers and editors were on strike.

One tidbit from this project stuck in my mind. During the strike, I interviewed a number of the *Times*'s journalists who were so angry and frustrated with the management of the newspaper that I asked them why they didn't quit and find work elsewhere.

Their response was one of incredulity. "Why would anyone leave *The New York Times*?" That was their uniform response!

Rosenthal liked the surveys we did with *Times* employees and saw their potential for conducting polls among the general public. The result was the *New York Times*/Yankelovich poll, which became a regular feature of the newspaper.

It lasted for years, until CBS offered its own polling capabilities to the *Times*, cutting their costs in half. It was an offer they couldn't refuse. We moved our firm's polling services to TIME, Inc., in the form of the *TIME/* Yankelovich survey, which lasted for an even longer period.

A second event that year was founding the nonprofit Public Agenda with Cyrus Vance.

Vance was a prominent New York attorney and public servant who had been secretary of the army and was to become secretary of state in the Carter administration.

Vance and I were friends. We used to meet for lunch once a month to talk politics. At one such lunch, in the winter of 1975, both of us expressed frustration that our political leadership seemed to be ignoring all of the truly urgent problems facing the nation.

We decided to try to do something about it.

At the time, both our political leaders and the press were hung up on a trivial diplomatic conflict between the United States and China. Taiwan and Mainland China both claimed ownership of two tiny islands in the straits of Formosa—Quemoy and Matsu. The United States sided with Taiwan, angering the Communist government of China.

Every day the media obsessed over the issue, reflecting our government's obsession and pushing into the background a raging stagflation and other thorny domestic issues that intruded on people's lives.

With the 1976 presidential campaign still in its planning stages, both Vance and I pondered what it would take to change the national conversation in time for the upcoming election. We felt that it would be useful to learn more about the voters' genuine concerns and to focus the attention of the presidential candidates on them.

We decided to develop a nonpartisan analysis of the issues that mattered most to voters—and strategies for dealing with them. We also discussed what it would take to make sure that both the Republican and Democratic presidential candidates were thoroughly briefed on how the public felt about these issues.

I told Vance that with modest funding I could produce the required research, but would want to do so within the framework of a neutral, nonpartisan, not-for-profit organization.

He told me he was confident that he could reach the candidates of both parties—Gerald Ford, the Republican president who was running for a full second term, and the Democratic candidate, whoever he might be. We felt that if our timing was good, we might be able to shift the focus of the campaign away from trivia such as Quemoy and Matsu onto the issues that really counted for voters.

By the end of our lunch, we had decided that we would start an ad hoc organization to accomplish these two tasks. (We intended to shut it down immediately after the 1976 election was over.) We also agreed that the new organization would take no positions and make no recommendations.

This lack of partisanship, we felt, would add to the organization's credibility with the two political parties. Instead of lobbying, we would confine ourselves to identifying and clarifying the issues that mattered most to voters.

We agreed to contribute $5,000 each to get the organization started and to hit up our friends for equal amounts. Within a month or so, we had raised more than $100,000, mostly in the form of $5,000 contributions from friends, and were ready to launch the research. We found some cheap office space in a small building on East 39th Street and staffed it with temp help.

I recruited a number of colleagues and other professionals who believed in the project and were willing to volunteer their thought and skills to the work. We called the new organization the Public Agenda.

By the end of the summer of 1976, the Public Agenda had produced three reports on the issues of greatest importance to voters.

Report #1: How to confront the severe stagflation that afflicted our economy—double-digit inflation alongside high levels of unemployment.

Report #2: How best to conduct our post-Vietnam foreign policy, especially in relationship to the cold war with the Soviet Union.

Report #3: How to restore and rebuild the nation's trust in our institutions and to revitalize voter confidence in the moral leadership of government.

All three reports were based on interviews with voters, experts, and leaders.

I had taken responsibility for producing the research. Vance took responsibility for seeing to it that the research findings reached the presidential candidates and were taken seriously by them.

I recently looked up these reports. Though written almost four decades ago, they stand up well. They identified three compelling issues for the 1976 presidential campaign, distilled how the general public as well as the nation's most respected experts across the political spectrum thought about them, and set forth strategies for dealing with them. They also preserved a tone of respect and impartiality for the views of both the voting public and the experts.

In the nationally televised presidential debates that followed, the candidates referred extensively to two of our three reports. President Ford made good use of our report on inflation and unemployment, and Jimmy Carter, the Democratic candidate, relied heavily on our foreign policy report. (When Carter became president, one of his first acts was to invite Cy Vance to become his secretary of state.)

We were so encouraged by the results that we began to rethink our earlier decision to close down the Public Agenda right after the election. The Ford Foundation gave us a small grant to conduct a survey among influential thought leaders on whether or not the Public Agenda should continue to clarify the public voice on nonelection as well as election issues. The responses to our inquiries were so positive and enthusiastic that we agreed to continue with the Public Agenda.

Vance promised that once he completed his stint as secretary of state he would return to the chairmanship of the Public Agenda, which he did. I agreed to continue on as its part-time president, which I did as well.

The act of founding is a special form of human creativity; the ancient Romans regarded it as sacred. I have always shared this reverence for initiating something that endures beyond one's lifespan. "To invest one's substance in forms of life and work that will outlive the self"—this is the statement that psychologist George Vaillant cites as the most succinct description of the phase of life that he and Erik Erikson called "generativity."[1] This is the stage of life when people start to fuss less with their own careers and to concern themselves more with caring for others, particularly the next generation.

I had started other entities, but founding the Public Agenda has come to hold a special meaning for me. The Public Agenda is dedicated to making our democracy work better through engaging the public in the truly important issues of the times. It conducts the kind of projects that would be difficult to carry out in a for-profit organization.

We founded the Public Agenda explicitly to bridge the huge divide that separates elites from average Americans. The Public Agenda was my first effort to translate into action some practical methods for narrowing that gap and for opening space for the public to participate in shaping policy.

Unfortunately, the current momentum of our society pushes toward *widening* the gap between America's elites and the general public, not narrowing it. There is little chance that it will narrow itself.

To my mind, the Public Agenda is just the kind of institution the nation needs to reboot our democracy.

Chapter Twenty-Six

The Elitist Double Whammy

Elites generally don't want to hear from the public. They may say that they do and may speak well of a government of, by, and for the people. But a characteristic of any elite organization is that it is composed of people who think well of themselves and don't feel they need input from others.

On the big decisions facing the nation, the public is rarely drawn into the action in ways that bring out the best in the American people—their practicality, thoughtfulness, generosity of spirit.

We Americans pride ourselves on being a less class-ridden society than the Brits or the French with their long histories of aristocrats flying high above mere commoners. But the disconnect separating average Americans from our own elites—experts, people of great wealth, business leaders, top professionals, academics from research universities, scientists, and bureaucrats—is as wide if not wider than the class divisions of old Europe.

Upwardly mobile Americans constantly seek superiority over others. Businesspeople do it through accumulating money and organizational authority; bureaucrats do it through expanding their sphere of power and control; experts do it through piling on credentials and specialized knowledge. Every elite subculture speaks and writes in its own specialized vocabulary.

Our society has assumed that no special effort is required to manage this elitist striving so that it *improves* the practice of democracy rather than stunts its development. Our Founding Fathers were remarkably insightful about other threats to democratic practice, but not about this one. And subsequent generations have seen no need to confront it and manage it in a better fashion.

Huge differences in expertise, education, income, and deeply ingrained attitudes of superiority all cut the electorate out of the loop on important policy decisions. Public ignorance then becomes a self-fulfilling prophecy:

by just *acting like* elites, elites help to insure that the public remains ignorant—and at the same time they use the public's ignorance as an excuse for excluding average citizens.

This double whammy is no secret. Everyone is aware of it, but our national pride makes us reluctant to face up to how very elitist our society has become. Instead of making a fuss about it, we resort to a simple-minded mythology, namely, that the public is not as well informed as it should be.

The solution is deemed to be "public education": give the public the information it needs and the disconnect will be magically repaired.

The obstinacy of this assumption never ceases to amaze me. Its persistence, decade after decade, in the face of overwhelming evidence to the contrary, is almost unfathomable. You could inundate the public with relevant information, and the disconnect would persist unchanged. Lack of information is not the problem.

Our society has succeeded in overcoming other threats to our democracy such as slavery, monopolistic concentrations of power, and gross gender inequality. But for a variety of reasons, it persists in ignoring the elite/public divide.

The Public Agenda revealed the ethical nature of this divide in one of the three reports it gave to the presidential candidates, Gerald Ford and Jimmy Carter, in 1975. The title of the report was *Moral Leadership in Government.*

Here are some of that report's main findings and conclusions:

- In the aftermath of Watergate, the war in Vietnam and an economy mired in stagnation, a majority of Americans had come to believe that our nation had wandered down the wrong track and that something was ethically wrong.[1]
- In discussing what that "something wrong" might be, average Americans referred to "the weakening of a sense of right and wrong in our public life" and to their concern that "our political leaders and national institutions no longer distinguish between right and wrong in the conduct of the public's business."[2]
- The public majority agreed with the statement that "the country has been trending toward a psychology of self-interest so all-embracing that no room is left for commitment to national and community interests."[3]
- The public also expressed the fear that our elites "have lost sight of any larger obligation to the public and are indifferent or worse to anything that does not benefit—immediately and directly—themselves or their institutions." Americans had come to fear that "the very meaning of the public good is disappearing, drowned in a sea of self-seeking."[4]
- From the public's perspective, the main symptoms of this loss of concern are: widespread unfairness; an erosion of respect for right and wrong; the spread of "aimlessness, purposelessness, selfishness and drift, reflecting

the lack of a clear vision of what this country stands for," and a failure to motivate elites to serve the public good.[5]

- The report concludes: "There is a hunger—and a mandate—for the top level of our political leadership to restore what people feel has been lost, to reaffirm the meaning of the public good, and to distinguish it as sharply as possible from the pursuit of private interests."[6]

It is interesting to observe that the ethical issues associated with today's wicked problems are not new. They plainly manifested themselves in the mid-1970s.

The report identified the elite ethical lapse as a failure to accept the *responsibilities* as well as the *privileges* that go with high social status. These responsibilities require that the elite segments of our society concern themselves with the larger social good, not just with their own self-interest and ego gratification.

One of the reasons European aristocracy was able to survive and prosper for so long was "noblesse oblige"—a tradition that great privilege carries equally great responsibilities.

Growing up as a poor boy in Boston and gaining access to the Boston Latin School and Harvard, I was a direct beneficiary of the strong sense of noblesse oblige that the Cabots, Lodges, Richardsons, Adams, Elliots, and other Boston Brahmins had developed over their long history. I had the good fortune to grow up in a city that had bred elites in the best tradition of old Europe.

What the American public was saying in the mid-1970s was that our elites enjoyed the privileges and advantages of an aristocracy, but lacked any counterbalancing ethical stewardship for the care and feeding of the public good.

To the extent that this criticism is valid, it is an ethical indictment that places the viability of our democracy in jeopardy. It may not threaten our survival, but it surely weakens our problem-solving capabilities.

In our technological era, we have a tendency to equate problem solving with finding technical fixes. If we could solve our nation's main problems—the growing defects in our form of capitalism, democracy, social norms, and culture—with technical fixes, we wouldn't have to depend on discovering a new philosophy of life.

I believe the opposite is true. I do not minimize the importance of technology. But I believe that it is becoming increasingly evident that however wonderful our technology may be, our most fundamental challenges are philosophical in nature.

We must do a far better job in setting priorities in values, pursuing greater fairness and equality of opportunity, and avoiding the immense varieties of crooked thinking that are threatening to overwhelm our society.

Chapter Twenty-Seven

Missed Chances to Regain the Public Trust

The Public Agenda has devoted decades of research to achieving a better understanding of how the public makes up its mind, especially on controversial issues. This research suggests that the elite/public disconnect distorts public opinion in four different ways, each one difficult to correct.

The first form of distortion comes from *mistrust*. The public mistrusts most of our institutions of governance.

In gauging the level of public mistrust, one polling item has proven particularly illuminating. Over many decades, public opinion polls have asked Americans: "How much do you trust the government to do the right thing most of the time?" (The interviewer asks the same question about other institutions, such as the Congress, the political parties, the military, banks, pharmaceutical companies, etc.)

The shifts in the public's responses to this revealing question could hardly be more dramatic. In the late fifties, a whopping 78 percent majority of Americans said they trusted government to do the right thing most of the time. That number plunged all the way to 20 percent in the 2010–2013 period.

A similar pattern holds true for other institutions such as Congress, the banks, and the two major political parties (but not the military, which has maintained the public's trust).

The second distortion comes from the public's *lack of engagement*. President Lyndon Johnson understood the high price politicians had to pay for this lack of engagement. When asked to explain why he insisted upon engaging a particularly obstreperous group of his critics, Johnson's explanation was as clear as it was crude. "I would rather," he said in his Texas drawl, "have them pissin' out from inside the tent than pissin' in from outside."

The majority of Americans are more polite and less vivid: they simply complain to pollsters that they do not have a significant voice in the decisions that affect their lives.

Our researchers sometimes have the opportunity to conduct daylong in-depth dialogues with citizens. As soon as the participants in the dialogues feel that they are being heard and taken seriously, their attitude shifts from one of skepticism and self-centeredness, to one of responsibility and concern for others as well as for themselves.

To play their part as responsible citizens, people have to feel that they are being invited to consult about matters of importance to their lives. One of the great changes initiated by our nation's cultural revolution was to make the public less dependent on the authority of institutions and leaders. Americans no longer accept authority automatically; they insist on having more say over their own lives and fortunes.

A third form of distortion comes from the public's suspicion that elites are operating from a *different set of values* because they think they are superior to regular people.

People support organizations such as the NRA and ACLU and movements such as the Tea Party and Occupy Wall Street out of resentment that self-righteous elites are trampling on their values and threatening to take their country away from them. This kind of resentment was strong in 1975 when we founded the Public Agenda; it is much stronger now, decades later.

The fourth source of distortion comes from *failure to provide citizens with special tools they need* to participate actively and intelligently in policy deliberation.

Over the years I have come to appreciate the usefulness of one particular tool. It formulates policy choices for public consideration and spells out the pros and cons of each choice in language that people can understand. When people are given real choices to consider, they find it a lot easier to make up their minds than when issues are defined from an expert point of view.

The Kettering Foundation calls this tool "choice work"—drawing out the consequences of various policy choices from the point of view of the moral and practical implications of each choice.

The ObamaCare legislation in 2009 engendered public mistrust and mis-understanding largely because this indispensable choice work task was over-looked. The public was never presented with a limited number of alternative choices, with their practical implications fully spelled out.

Critics framed the consequences of ObamaCare in scare terms: "death panels" and "rationing."

If its *supporters* had taken the trouble to lay out the choices for public deliberation, with their consequences and trade-offs made explicit, and had used this framing to engage the public, our health care system might now be less of a monster whose out-of-control costs threaten to engulf our economy.

What a huge difference there is between the simplistic view that the elite/ public gap can be overcome merely through "informing the public" and the insight that the disconnect goes far deeper. It reflects mistrust, a failure of engagement, differences in values, and a lack of indispensible policy tools for cultivating public judgment.

The task of addressing these flaws is formidable.

Chapter Twenty-Eight

Coming to Public Judgment

Over and over again, our research has demonstrated that public opinion evolves through distinct stages as it makes its awkward climb up the public Learning Curve from mushy raw opinion to settled public judgment. This is a process that can take great lengths of time depending on the strength of the public's resistance.

As reported in an earlier chapter, the Learning Curve typically evolves through three stages:

1. Stage One: Consciousness raising to create public awareness of an issue.
2. Stage Two: Confronting and working through emotional resistances such as denial, prejudice, and wishful thinking.
3. Stage Three: Reaching cognitive and emotional resolution.

Figure 28.1 represents a typical learning curve.

In the past, strong and forceful public opinion has been a key factor in our nation's history of successful problem solving. The American public is more results-oriented and less ideological than our nation's elites. The public is often willing to brush aside ideological purity in favor of what works. At one time, the productive interplay between our ideologically oriented elites and a pragmatic public gave our democracy a lot of problem-solving horsepower.

That interplay has eroded over a period of decades. Our elites have lost touch with the public. They are mired in serious misconceptions about how average Americans make up their minds. These misconceptions distort their thinking, leading to mutual estrangement.

Listed below are the main misconceptions that distort elite thinking about how the public makes up its mind, and how to correct them:

■ SUBSTITUTE THE CONCEPT OF THE "PUBLIC'S LEARNING CURVE" FOR THAT OF AN "INFORMED PUBLIC"

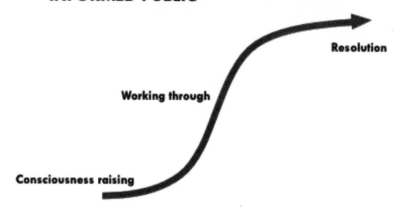

Figure 28.1.

Misconception: The public makes up its mind when exposed to factual information and/or arguments in favor or against a course of action.
Correction: Facts are often a secondary—and even minor—influence on how people make up their minds. Far more important is how well policy ideas fit into people's preexisting belief systems and values. Media-conveyed information counts primarily in stage one of the *Learning Curve. Media influence is far less important in the other two stages.*

Misconception: The public makes up its mind in real time once it has the relevant information it needs.
Correction: The public rarely resolves controversial issues when first exposed to relevant information. Typically, people need months, years, or decades to make up their minds, however compelling and extensive the facts may be (e.g., climate change).
The journalistic assumption is that factual information, absorbed at the same time it is transmitted, is the key to firm public opinion. This cliché is almost ludicrous because it is so far from the truth. Yet it persists decade after decade, impervious to the overwhelming evidence against it.

Misconception: Elites and average voters share similar belief systems and frameworks. We are all Americans. Once voters are properly "educated," they tend to agree with the conclusions of their elite leaders.
Correction: The public's values, attitudes, and interests are rarely the same as those of elites, and therefore their frameworks differ starkly. The two groups

may arrive at very different conclusions despite having access to the same information.

The dominance of these misconceptions means that elites often relate to the public in ways that breed confusion, resentment, and mistrust. This makes it difficult for sound public judgment to form. And when public judgment is lacking, unsolved problems fester.

Chronic joblessness, slow growth, failure to confront climate change, faulty education practices, out-of-control institutions, eroding infrastructure, unsustainable medical costs, unmanageable budget deficits—the list of problems that suffer neglect because of the lack of mature public judgment is mind-boggling.

Elite opinion and public opinion work best when they are mutually supportive, correcting each other's flaws and reinforcing each other's strengths. Designing the optimum relationship between elites and public in a democracy is a huge unsolved challenge.

The Founding Fathers gave exquisite attention to a related problem—preventing the aggregation of excessive power in any one branch of government. The system of checks and balances they designed continues to function effectively. But they dealt only superficially with managing relations between elites and average citizens.

We need new attitudes and new institutions to build mutually supportive relationships between our elites and the public. Standing alone, each side is prone to a variety of ills.

Elites grow arrogant, isolated, overly specialized, and prisoners of groupthink. They fall into all manner of traps. The ironic title of David Halberstam's book *The Best and the Brightest* aptly captures the folly of the elites who escalated the war in Vietnam. The historian Barbara Tuchman's book *The March of Folly* depicts the disastrous elite decision making in WWI. Other books recount the irresponsibility of decision making by financial elites leading to the Great Recession of 2008–2009.

The general public is vulnerable as well. Their traps include wishful thinking; procrastination, denial, lack of imagination, ignorance, avoidance of cognitive dissonance, naïveté, blind conviction, prejudice, distraction by trivia: the list is daunting.

Working in closer harmony with each other, elites and the public can reduce each other's limitations and augment each other's strengths. To restore our democratic problem-solving capabilities, we need to forge better elite/public alliances.

To be sure, there will always be elites who care only for their own interests and don't give a damn about the public good. But most of our elites do care. And we need them for their political leadership, knowledge, economic innovation, moral vision, and stewardship. These strengths form a bulwark against the limitations of the public's understanding.

We also need a better understanding of the public's distinctive *ways of knowing*. We need to learn how to help average Americans align their choices more faithfully with our society's core values. In my decades of conducting public opinion surveys, I developed great respect for the nonscientific ways of knowing that the public uses to arrive eventually at wise judgments, but that experts scorn and deride.

At the very least, on every important issue we need to understand whether the public is at the beginning, in the middle, or moving toward the end of the Learning Curve process. What obstacles are preventing it from moving to the next stage? What can be done to reduce or remove them? When the public does reach the end stage, what shape is its judgment likely to take?

The concept of "public judgment" that I have defined and described in several books refers to the end product of the Learning Curve.[1] Public judgment differs from raw opinion in three ways—stability, consistency, and acceptance of consequences.

When people reach judgment on an issue, the views they hold become stable and do not change even when pollsters change the wording of questions. They also become free of contradictions and inconsistencies. Most importantly, people who arrive at sound judgment come to accept the full consequences of their views (e.g., if you support capital punishment, you accept the possibility that innocent people may be put to death).

Sooner or later, I expect that this picture of public judgment will become more widely accepted. It is likely to do so because the evidence for it is so compelling. But the convictions of journalists run deep, as does their resistance to examining them.

Here, once again, we find a major distortion buried in the tacit frameworks of an elite profession. This distortion has a crippling effect on the day-to-day practice of democracy in America. It robs our elites of their ability to understand the true nature of public opinion and what it takes to cultivate sound public judgment.

Chapter Twenty-Nine

Losing the Battle with the News Media

Here is a vivid example from my personal experience of the depth of the news media's resistance to adopting a less oversimplified, more nuanced understanding of how the public goes about making up its mind on issues.

In February 1979, I published an article in *Foreign Affairs* magazine focusing on how easy it was to misunderstand American attitudes toward other nations. "Since few foreign policy issues are ever discussed thoroughly with the public," I concluded, "it follows that what public opinion polls measure is usually what the public believes *prior* to having considered a foreign policy issue in depth."[1]

For example, it was only after considerable public discussion that the American public changed its mind in support of, rather than opposition to, proposed Panama Canal treaties.

I argued that foreign governments could be dangerously misled if they took our raw public opinion poll numbers at face value. And so could our own government.

I urged the journalism and polling professions to develop ways to signal its readers when public opinion on an issue was still raw and in a formative stage and when it was solid and firm and could be counted on not to shift around wildly.

Shortly after the article was published, our firm decided to take the initiative. We proposed to our client, *TIME Magazine*, that they add a new feature to their ongoing *TIME*/Yankelovich surveys. We met with Henry Grunwald, *TIME*'s editor-in-chief, to try to persuade him that public opinion polling had a defect that was preventing journalists and readers from correctly interpreting poll findings on many controversial subjects. We proposed a way for *TIME* to address and correct the defect.

Grunwald paid close attention as we explained that you cannot tell simply from looking at a poll's findings whether people had really made up their minds on an issue. We proposed to Grunwald that *TIME* sponsor the development of a new poll feature that would tell readers whether the public's views on vital issues were firm or volatile, especially on foreign policy.

"Oh," said Henry, who was a quick study. "You want to develop a mushiness index. Good idea. How long will it take and how much will it cost?"

Having worked with Grunwald in the past, I wasn't at all surprised by his openness and receptivity to new ideas. We left the meeting with authorization to proceed with the development of what we thereafter always referred to as the Mushiness Index.

We were full of respect for Grunwald, especially when he said that he would treat the index as a public service, available to anyone and everyone who wanted to use it.

In the next few months, we developed a simple-to-use index. Grunwald had warned us that if we came up with something too complicated, his writers wouldn't use it because it would get in their way in reporting stories.

Florence Skelly suggested that once we found a low-cost way to test the firmness of answers to poll questions, we simply attach an asterisk to poll answers that were clearly "mushy." In that way, readers could tell at a glance whether the public had genuinely made up its mind or whether the issue was still in play.

In developing the Mushiness Index, we first conducted an extensive literature search and then did three pilot tests on the battery of questions that would make up the index. Once we had settled on the index questions, we tested them out in a special survey. The survey included a range of controversial foreign policy issues:

- selling arms to Communist China,
- establishing diplomatic relations with Castro's Cuba,
- cutting military aid to Israel,
- giving military support to anti-Communist nations that violate human rights,
- using military force to insure reliable sources of oil,
- reestablishing normal relations with Iran, and
- increasing our defense spending to insure military superiority over the Soviet Union.

We also included a number of controversial domestic issues, such as building more nuclear power plants, conducting sex education in high schools, restricting immigration into the United States, and making all abortions illegal.

In March 1981, we presented our findings to *TIME* and described how the index was developed and tested.[2] True to his word, Grunwald recommended the index to his writers and called a press conference inviting other publications and polling organizations to use it in whatever way they wished, as open-source, noncompetitive material.

Everything went smoothly, according to plan. Except for one small problem. *To my knowledge, no one ever accepted the invitation to use the Mushiness Index, including Grunwald's own journalists!* Not our client, *TIME*. Not any other publication or polling organization. No one criticized it. No one said it was wrong. Or useless. Or unnecessary. Or a waste of time and resources.

It just didn't catch on.

I have never fully understood all of the reasons for its sad fate. At least one reason is that it required *somewhat greater expenditure of money and effort*.

Public opinion polls are expensive to conduct. To ascertain whether a respondent's answer is firm or mushy, you have to ask some additional questions (e.g., how personally engaged respondents are with the issue, how extensively they discuss it with others, how easy or difficult it would be for them to change their minds). Journalists and media management must have felt that the value added by the index wasn't worth the extra cost and effort needed to *explain* it as well as to use it.

Another source of resistance was its implicit criticism of poll reliability. Pollsters were uneasy about any innovation that implied that you can't always rely on poll results. In promoting the Mushiness Index, we were complicating life for everyone: the pollsters conducting the polls, the clients who paid the costs, the journalists reporting the results, and the public struggling to understand what the polls meant.

I was well aware of its added costs and need for explanation. I never felt that it should be used routinely on all issues. But I did feel that it was well worth the extra effort on high-stakes issues that might prove exceptionally mushy.

This is just one tiny example of how badly out of sync the culture of journalism is from the complexities and nuances of the public's Learning Curve. It would be a far more convenient world for journalists if the public wasn't so ornery about how it goes about making up its mind.

Chapter Thirty

How My Philosophy for Living Evolved

Over a period of years, my work shifted from marketing research to tracking the nation's cultural revolution to focusing on the role of the public voice in shaping our democracy.

Throughout this latter phase, I constantly kept bumping up against the realization that two powerful forces were colliding, leading to a serious dysfunction in our democracy.

Our news media is one of the two forces; the public voice is the other.

Our news media do an outstanding job in carrying out their mission, as they conceive it. But that mission is focused too narrowly on current "news." This doesn't meet our democracy's need to engage citizens in a thoughtful manner in the great issues that confront our society, especially when these issues grow "wicked."

The most obvious corrective strategy would be to broaden the functions of the news media so that they address stages two and three of the Learning Curve as well as stage one. Or new institutions could be developed to attend to these two stages. But the likelihood of either happening within a reasonable time span seems zilch.

A more practical strategy would put more of a burden on the public itself rather than on our elite institutions. I think we should strive to encourage a critical mass of our citizens to adopt a philosophy for living that gives as much importance to our society's flourishing as we now give to individual flourishing.

The starting point for any serious philosophy for living must be an understanding of what matters most in life. But achieving that understanding is not easy. Individuals need a lot of guidance to succeed in doing so.

Chapter 30

It should be the role of culture to give that guidance. But our cultural revolution has proven so decentering to our society that, at least for now, our culture cannot provide people with the help they need to make the right existential life decisions for themselves.

If the culture cannot provide such guidance, people will have to provide it for themselves. I am convinced that the best way to do so is for individuals to make the effort to develop their own philosophy for living.

My own philosophy for living evolved through four phases.

BEWILDERMENT

In the first phase, as a freshman at Harvard, I had discovered philosophy as if it were a vast fount of wisdom. But when I returned to Harvard after three years of military service, I found that philosophy, as I had thought of it, had changed in ways I found unpalatable.

I was at a loss to understand how my respected professors had come to lead the entire department down what seemed to me a self-destructive, barren, unbeautiful path. After struggling with the change, both as an undergraduate and as a graduate student, I abandoned my plan to become a professor of philosophy—but not my interest in philosophy.

THE SEARCH FOR ANSWERS

Phase two was my search for the reason philosophy had taken such an alien turn.

For years, I kept searching for the causes of philosophy's wrong turn (as I conceived it). Why would a discipline with several thousand years of experience wander so mindlessly down a wrong path without stirring up much protest or rebellion from within? I had to find how and why something so unusual—and remarkable—had taken place.

Ultimately, I did find answers in the writings of a few insightful philosophers, answers that had a major influence on my evolving philosophy of life.

HARM TO OTHER SUBJECTS

In phase three I became aware that the same narrow and destructive framework that had thrown academic philosophy off course was doing comparable damage to other subjects, particularly psychoanalysis and the social sciences.

I decided to dig more deeply into how the prevailing "scientism" of the era had wrapped psychoanalysis and other social sciences in its tentacles, crushing the life out of them.

THE PRESENT

I am now in the fourth and current phase of the evolution of my philosophy for living. This phase focuses on the importance of drawing together the various strands of what I have learned both from my professional work and my personal life experience.

I am only one of a vast number of Americans who believe that our society suffers a huge loss when the ancient tradition of philosophy is pursued only by scholars and is locked up exclusively as an academic subject in our colleges and universities.

The raw materials for people's philosophy for living can come from a variety of sources. Philosophy's trove of writings is just one source. Personal experience is another. The findings of science about human nature and thought are another. And cultural values are yet another.

The relative importance of each of these sources will vary, reflecting the individual's interests and history. (For example, traditional philosophy played a disproportionately large role in my own life.) But my surmise is that the philosophies for living of most Americans will turn out to share a great deal in common.

In what follows, I trace the evolution of my own philosophy for living through the phases noted above.

III

My Philosophy for Living

Chapter Thirty-One

Dinner with Quine

I began searching for an explanation of the bleak turn taken by academic philosophy while I was still in graduate school. I was particularly interested in one faculty philosopher, Willard Van Orman Quine.

Professor Quine, then a promising young assistant professor in the philosophy department, eventually became one of the world's most outstanding logicians, in the grand tradition of famous Harvard philosophers.

As an undergraduate, I had taken a number of courses with Quine in logic and in the philosophy of language. He was the most concise thinker I had ever met. He could express in a single sentence what others would take paragraphs to say. He was an artist of thought and language, a Picasso of verbal expression, conveying complex thoughts in the most parsimonious manner possible. He was, moreover, a friendly and agreeable person with a warm smile, though he often seemed a bit remote—at least to me as a student.

I suspected that Quine and his work might harbor the answer to the question that most bewildered me. What, I wondered, was the relationship between "logic" as a tool of reasoning and discovering answers to the existential question of how to live? If applying logic provided valid answers, Quine, the virtuoso of logic, would surely show me how to connect the tool of logic to the Socratic question of how to live the good life.

I took every course in philosophy that Professor Quine gave. I was determined to grasp the nature of logic as philosophy's main analytic tool. There was something about logic I vaguely mistrusted. Yet I was sure I would eventually find clarity (and hopefully, a renewed confidence in academic philosophy) if I continued to follow Quine's deep probings.

Quine's various courses in advanced logic culminated in a course called Mathematical Logic 19B, a seminar I took with five other graduate students, all foreign exchange students. Mothersill was Canadian, Craig was German, Myhill was English, Hisch was Polish, and Wang was Chinese. I have always found it odd that though I often forget the names of people I have known for decades, I have never forgotten the names, faces, and personalities of the tiny, ill-assorted hodgepodge of philosophy graduate students who gathered around Willard Van Orman Quine, exploring the mysteries of Mathematical Logic 19B.

I had taken so many of his courses that Quine and I had developed a personal relationship, and I was thrilled when he invited me to dinner. I spent most of the week before the date of our dinner thinking about how to ask him the very personal question that was on the top of my mind. The trick would be to phrase it so that it wouldn't come across as a criticism of him as a person.

After dinner, sitting out on his porch on a warm Cambridge July night, I screwed up my courage and said to him, "Van, I hope you won't mind if I ask you a personal question—not to pry into your life but to help me with a decision I'm about to make."

He said, "Sure," and poured both of us another cup of coffee.

"Well," I said, drawing a deep breath, "Here goes."

I said, "I'd like to give you my reasons for my losing interest in philosophy, and I want to know whether I have drawn the right or wrong inferences from what I've learned from your courses."

"So many disciplines have broken away from philosophy," I said, "that it hasn't been left with much distinctively its own." Logical reasoning is philosophy's only remaining proprietary tool. When philosophers argue with one another and logically prove that one or the other position is wrong, they are in pursuit of truth.

Now you and other logicians, I said, are depriving philosophy of the one method left to it: the tool of logic. You, along with Russell and Whitehead, have demonstrated that *logic by itself adds no new knowledge or information about the world.*

Sure, logic may be useful in helping us to clarify our thinking and perform other mental operations. But by itself logical reasoning can never lead to truths about the nature, purpose, and meaning of life and its values.

I told Van that I had found his boldness in exploring the foundations of math and logic to be one of the most impressive intellectual feats I'd ever encountered, but that at least for me personally, it led to a bleak conclusion.

It had put the final nail in the coffin of philosophy.

Van Quine sipped his coffee quietly.

I plowed ahead. The history of philosophy, I said, has been one long process of stripping philosophy of its unique methods for gaining knowledge, insight, and wisdom about life. If this is true, what is left? Why would anyone want to devote his life to the remnants?

And here I came to my personal questions. "Am I even approximately correct in my inference? And if so, why do you, Van Quine, continue to work in the field of philosophy?"

For a long time, Quine did not answer.

Finally, he did speak. He thanked me for grouping him with towering figures like Russell and Whitehead and said modestly that he didn't see himself as having that sort of stature. He said he thought my summary was overstated, that there was much that remained distinctive to philosophy.

But he went on to say that no one could disagree that philosophy's grand pretensions of the past had been radically diminished.

Speaking for himself personally, he said philosophy continued to interest him. He had discovered he had a flair for it, and a career in Harvard's philosophy department suited his temperament extremely well.

At the end of that memorable evening, I thanked him, left his house, strolled back to my apartment in a bemused state, and, at the end of that semester, left Harvard and academic philosophy forever.

Many years later, shortly before Quine died, I visited him at the Harvard Faculty Club. I believe he was over ninety years old at the time of my visit. He still had the same warm, shy smile. We spoke cordially for a few minutes. I recalled his statement that his career at Harvard had suited him well, and I realized how right he had been about himself.

Several years ago, I had occasion to open my Quine textbook for Mathematical Logic19B. The book opened to page 205 that I had underlined and annotated as a student.

Here is a reproduction of part of page 205:

§ 37 A B S T R A C T I O N O F R E L A T I O N S 205
The following definition is accordingly adopted.
D26. p ÿ _q or pÿ _q for p ^ _ ^ _(_(_, _))q.
The following theorem and metatheorem reveal positions from
which the dot is suppressible. †436. (x)(y)(z) ÿ x(y, z) _ x(y, z).
Proof. _433 (& D26) ÿ x(y, z) _ y, z_ V x(y, z)_100 (& D24) _ x(y, z)
_437. pÿ ^ ^ _ = ^ ^ _q.Proof. Case I: _ is not _.
_433, _188 p ^ ^ _ L433 = ^ ^ _ R433q_100, _188 (& D25) = ^ ^ _q. (1)
_171 (& D26) p 1 _ 437 q.Case 2: _ is _. Let and_ be new and distinct.
_137, _188 (& D25) p ^ ^ _ = ^ _(9 _)(_, _ _ V _ = _;_ _)q
_234b, _188 (& D25) = ^ ^(_ _ =)q (1)_437 (Case 1) = ÿ ^ ^(_ _ =)q
(1), _227 = ÿ ^ ^ _q.

I could have reproduced virtually any other paragraph or page in Quine's 331-page book,[1] and it would look pretty much the same. Most of the book now strikes me as incomprehensible.

Since the Enlightenment, logical reasoning has reigned supreme in the culture of the West, claiming primacy over other ways of knowing grounded in faith, intuition, imagination, and feelings. The claims of reason and rationality, personified by logic, science, and scientism, have dominated our intellectual lives.

The limitations of logic are the limitations of reason and rationality. I concluded that I wasn't likely to learn much about how to live from continuing to focus on the role of logic in finding truth.

Ironically, it was a puff of logic that nailed the issue for me:

> Logic doesn't reveal anything new or interesting about life.
> What drew me to philosophy and logic was finding something new and interesting about life.
> Ergo, *au revoir*, logic.

Chapter Thirty-Two

How Scientism Nearly Devoured Philosophy

My personal goal has always been to gain a better understanding of *human* truths. Though I abandoned academic philosophy because it failed to engage those kinds of truths, I never felt that I was walking away from philosophy itself. Rather, I felt that academic philosophy had disowned its own great heritage.

If the kind of American pragmatism that had flourished in the United States prior to World War II had retained a vigorous presence in our universities, philosophy might have maintained its vitality. But within philosophy departments like those at Harvard, Yale, and Princeton, the kind of pragmatism associated with William James and John Dewey had come to be regarded as old-fashioned, obsolete, and softheaded, an object of ridicule for the hardheaded positivists and logicians who dominated the scene.

As I had complained to Van Quine, philosophy had become preoccupied with the nature of scientific knowledge and logic rather than with seeking truths of living. Psychology and the other social sciences also had fallen under the sway of *scientism*—the assumption that science is the one and only path to legitimate knowledge.

Scientism had developed slowly over a long period of years. Philosophers were among the first to grasp the significance of scientific discovery and the power of the scientific method. A deep appreciation of the potential of scientific knowledge for advancing human well-being is very different from scientism, with its rejection of all ways of knowing except science.

Philosopher Alfred North Whitehead displays the deep appreciation perspective. Speaking of Galileo's pioneering work, he wrote, "Not since a babe was born in a manger was so momentous an event ushered in with so little stir."[1] The event to which Whitehead refers is the *birth of science*.

Measurement, experimentation, and theory took over from philosophy's armchair speculations about nature, launching science on a career whose momentum continues to gather force centuries later.

But by the twentieth century, some philosophers used science as a stick with which to beat up philosophy. That is *scientism,* and it came to dominate Anglo-American philosophy. Many logically minded philosophers held pre-scientific philosophies in contempt and ridicule. Bertrand Russell had the grace to refer to classical philosophical texts as "splendidly imaginative systems."

Russell wrote that ethical and religious motives had become "a hindrance to philosophy and ought to be put aside by those who wish to discover philosophical truth. . . . It is from science rather than from ethics and religion that philosophy should draw its aspirations."[2]

Other less tactful logicians referred to pre-twentieth-century philosophical systems in terms such as "adolescent," "worthless speculation," and "meaningless metaphysical nonsense."[3]

Philosophy, they said, had pursued many goals in its long history. But we now know, they said, that science is the only effective method for pursuing knowledge. We must, therefore, rid philosophy of all traces of unscientific thinking such as mysticism, sentimentality, religiosity, metaphysics, and ethical values. Scientism is the dogmatic refusal to see truth and virtue in any form of thought and inquiry except science.

The pernicious added assumption that the scientific strategy for investigating the natural world must also be good for understanding the human condition was accepted as a legitimate inference with practically no controversy.

When I was studying philosophy, the power and influence of scientism was at its peak. Ludwig Wittgenstein, one of the boldest philosophical thinkers, had concluded in the early years of his career in philosophy that we had reached *the end of philosophy.* He argued that there are only two forms of valid knowledge—empirical and logical. The first belongs to science. The second is really a form of analysis closely linked to mathematics.

There is, he deduced, no space left for philosophy as the quest for the truths of human living.

This meant, he believed, that philosophy must now narrow its boundaries, forsaking its own rich and sprawling history. It must disown metaphysics for its unscientific murkiness. It must dismiss the branches of philosophy concerned with ethics, aesthetics, theology, and metaphysics as mere forms of emotional expression ("emotional noise" as some called it derisively).

This logic led many to reject the work of the great nineteenth-century Continental philosophers like Hegel, Nietzsche, and Kierkegaard as well as leading twentieth-century Continental thinkers like Sartre and Heidegger.

Academic philosophy departments held these towering figures in contempt and in many instances refused to impart their teachings to their students.

The zeitgeist of scientism had first expressed itself in academic philosophy in Vienna in the 1920s and 1930s.

It appeared in the form of a narrow but powerful ideology called "logical positivism," which evolved into the more sophisticated but still narrow school of "analytic philosophy." In that form, scientism came to dominate the most prestigious academic departments of philosophy in the great research universities of both Britain and the United States.

It wasn't until the 1980s that philosophy began finally to liberate itself from analytic philosophy's deadly dominance. The controversial philosopher Richard Rorty led the charge.

In 1982, Rorty wrote a merciless critique of analytic philosophy.

Analytic philosophers were confident, Rorty wrote, that their method would inspire an "unprecedented era of cooperation, team work and agreement," leading to spectacular progress matching that of the natural sciences.

Yet, instead of consensus, Rorty argued, it created dissent, disagreement, and disorder everywhere—a jungle of competing interests.

Rorty described most contemporary philosophy departments as "a hodgepodge determined mostly by the accidents of power struggles within universities." He denounced the scientific pretensions of analytic philosophers as particularly bogus—unless, he added scornfully, "scientific means argumentative." In response to their claims to wisdom, Rorty compared analytic philosophers to a bunch of quarrelsome lawyers.

In his 1982 paper, Rorty concluded that decades of analytic philosophy had left the discipline in a state of disrepair—its premises unfounded, its consequences destructive, and the hubris of its leading thinkers ludicrous. Rorty faulted analytic philosophy for failing at every one of the goals and aspirations it set for itself![4]

Several years ago, I read Richard Rorty's book *Philosophy and Social Hope*. I smiled in sympathy with his statement that he had spent more than forty years wondering what philosophy was good for—without being able to articulate a coherent answer.

He writes, "When I am asked (as, alas, I often am) what I take the contemporary philosopher's mission or task to be, I get tongue-tied. The best I can do is stammer that we philosophy professors are people with a certain familiarity with a certain intellectual tradition." He adds lamely, "I do not want, however, to argue that philosophy is socially useless."[5]

Not exactly a ringing endorsement of philosophy's function.

I have often wondered whether Rorty would have found a better answer if he had abandoned academic philosophy altogether. He came close to doing so. In the last two decades of his life, he deftly managed to remove himself from university philosophy departments to a vaguely defined roving professorship in the humanities at the University of Virginia.

Once Rorty launched his critique of analytic philosophy, others followed. Not all subsequent critiques and commentaries shared Rorty's withering scorn, but most of them come to the same damning conclusion.

Six years after Rorty's brutal critique, philosophy professor Richard Bernstein of the New School for Social Research in New York presented a far more balanced judgment. Where Rorty was a warrior, Bernstein was a peacemaker, eager to build bridges of mutual understanding among the various warring factions in philosophy.

Yet despite this difference in tone and temperament, Bernstein's appraisal is remarkably similar to Rorty's. He concludes that despite some good work by individual practitioners, analytic philosophy has morphed into an untenable ideology, encouraging a counterproductive "adversarial" and "confrontational" style of argumentation.[6]

Bernstein complains that if college students wish to learn the teachings of some of the great Continental philosophers like "Hegel, Nietzsche, Kierkegaard and Heidegger," they have to leave philosophy for other departments such as religion and literature.[7]

In a softer tone, philosophy professor Kenneth R. Seeskin of Northwestern University offers a lamentation from the heart—a sad conviction that something has grown seriously amiss in philosophy and that analytic philosophy is the cause of it.[8]

Seeskin deplores that to get published, philosophers must present their work in a falsely scientific format full of "codes, symbols, and dialects incomprehensible to those outside the profession and not much better known to some of those inside." He regretfully notes that academic philosophers no longer focus on the great historic themes of the purpose and meaning of life and the nature of virtue.

The truly troublesome question for Seeskin is: "*What has become of that [which] once made philosophy majestic among human studies? At present, the subject appears to be without a center of gravity*" (emphasis added).[9]

To me, Seeskin's conclusion conveys a grave sense of loss.

Some of Harvard's leading philosophers, such as John Rawls, Hilary Putnam, and Stanley Cavell, have demonstrated that philosophy at Harvard is no longer the rigid and narrowly focused department of my youth. But the critiques of Seeskin, Rorty, Bernstein, and other philosophers bolstered my self-confidence in my judgment that philosophy had grown inhospitable to those of us interested in following Socrates' injunction to live the examined life.

Yet philosophy's belated rejection of scientism did not resolve the concern that had nagged at me for so many years: what had permitted philosophy to be taken over for such a long time by such an outlandish and implausible ideology as positivism?

And more personally: *could I rely on thinking philosophically for my own guidance in putting first things first?*

I was startled when part of the answer to these nagging questions came one weekend morning out of the blue.

It was a desultory rereading of Whitehead's *Science and the Modern World* one snowy Sunday morning that suddenly made me sit bolt upright. I was reading a section I had read before, but this time it conveyed a vivid new meaning for me.

Whitehead was writing about the most common fallacies to which philosophers are prone. Scientists and philosophers, he observed, don't always realize the extent to which the focus of their attention may not be realities but merely their own high-level abstractions.

Here, I realized, was the key to how the positivists and analytic philosophers had led philosophy into its wrong turn. The positivists had pounced upon abstractions useful in describing the natural world but futile in helping us to understand human experience. And they treated these abstractions as if they were objective realities, part of the "givens" of the universe.

It was their own highly selective frameworks, not scientific reality that had led them to reduce the sprawling field of philosophy to a narrow and arcane technical discipline.

Chapter Thirty-Three

My Wrong Map Problem

Once I came to understand what had driven philosophy down the wrong track, I was free to write the book I had been yearning to tackle for years. I was eager to apply what I had learned from philosophy's flirtation with scientism to my own research and to the disciplines that supported it such as psychology.

As French philosopher Merleau-Ponty observed, confining yourself to the conception of reality implied by science is like mistaking a map of a country you have never seen for the country itself; a map, furthermore, that depicts only the physical contours of the country and ignores its customs, its politics, its history, its weather, and its culture. A map is a very useful device, but one should not make the elementary mistake of assuming that only the map exists.

When it comes to scientific knowledge, we have learned to trust the sorts of maps that science provides. But scientific knowledge is a relatively small subset of the knowledge we need to exist, survive, know how to live right, and be wise.

For knowledge that lies outside the scientific domain, we have an incredibly wide number and variety of maps to choose among.

My psychology studies in graduate school had provided me with lots of examples of psychology being twisted out of shape in deference to the dictates of science. Almost every branch of psychology was burdened with obsolete philosophical frameworks that were slowing the field's progress or blocking it altogether.

Moreover, most psychologists had no desire to tackle the philosophical underpinnings of their subject.

Up to the end of the nineteenth century, psychology had actually been a branch of philosophy. The first modern psychologists felt an exhilarating freedom in being liberated from their philosophical shackles to become part of science. The last thing they wanted to do was to look backward. Philosophy be damned. Science was now the name of the game.

Having a foot in each world, philosophy and psychology, gave me a useful perspective. While not unique, it was different enough from the prevailing academic mind-set to present an opportunity for fresh thinking.

I was astonished at the degree to which unacknowledged philosophical assumptions were shaping the direction of psychological research, mostly to ill effect.

Sigmund Koch, a prominent psychologist of that era, ended his monumental seven-volume work, *Psychology: A Study of a Science*, with the conclusion that no other field has ever been "so harried by the shining success story of the older sciences [with its] stipulation that psychology be adequate to science outweighing its commitment that it be adequate to man."[1]

The purpose of a framework is to *enhance* the capabilities of a discipline, not weaken it. But the philosophical frameworks most psychologists now embraced were actually undermining their effectiveness.

I felt that if I could sketch out a more useful philosophical framework for one or another branch of psychology, I would be contributing something positive and perhaps even important to both fields.

The branch of psychology where philosophy exercised its most pervasive—and pernicious—influence was known as *behaviorism*. Seen from a philosophical point of view, behaviorism was an extreme instance of the distortions caused by scientism.

Psychologists who identified themselves as behaviorists worked mostly with rats rather than people. Their model of pure science was tracking the behavior of rats in mazes as the rats were either rewarded with food pellets or punished with electric shocks. One of its most influential advocates, psychologist E. C. Tolman, stated that "everything important in psychology . . . can be investigated in essence through the continued experimental and theoretical analysis of the determiners of rat behavior at a choice point in a maze."[2]

This mind-set faithfully reflected the agenda of those philosophers who were obsessed with scientism. They wanted to convert all branches of science into limited and precise sets of empirically testable statements. These would be verifiable through rigorous scientific experiments and measurements.

I spent a number of weekends absorbing the behaviorist literature and taking notes for a book, until I gradually realized that I was on the wrong track. While behaviorism fell squarely in the target zone I had selected, deconstructing it would be an exercise in futility.

I had no interest in writing a polemical tract, especially one that was likely to have zero impact. The behaviorists approached their subject with ideological zeal. They were true believers. Nothing that I had to say was likely to make the slightest dent in their beliefs or methods.

It was back to the drawing board for me.

If behaviorism and its positivist framework were the wrong point of entry into my chosen target zone, perhaps I could find a better one. The idea of writing a book on how philosophy could contribute positively to psychology was sound. The key was to find the right branches of philosophy and psychology to connect with each other.

Chapter Thirty-Four

A Look at Existentialism

The more I reflected on it, the more frequently existentialism kept popping up as a philosophy that might be well suited to psychology. I wondered whether existentialism might yield an alternative to the positivist/analytic framework.

A thriving school of existentialist psychiatry had grown up in Europe, explicitly grounded on the work of existentialist philosophers, most famously Jean-Paul Sartre.

In its concern with states of being such as loneliness, alienation, and *angst*, existentialism was at least focused on people rather than on maze-crazed rodents.

As I reread Sartre, I came to realize that his thought was largely derivative of Martin Heidegger. Indeed, most existentialist writers had found Heidegger impossible to avoid, and their work depended heavily on his reflections.

One of the leaders of the existential psychiatry movement, Dr. Henri Ellenberger, had written that Heidegger's work constituted "one of the greatest philosophical achievements of all times."[1] Could any endorsement be more fervent and compelling than that!

With a sinking feeling, I knew that sooner or later I would have to tackle Heidegger. I had put off doing so because I realized that it would be a dreadful chore. I was not comfortable reading Heidegger in German and had heard that English translations of his work were notoriously bad. Translated quotes from Heidegger's work were invariably dense and prickly.

Eventually, I forced myself to buy a copy of his early masterpiece, *Being and Time* (1927). I got bogged down almost immediately. At least three more times I picked it up and tried to read it, but got no further than page five. It was most discouraging. Nothing could have been more remote from my day-to-day concerns at the time than the ponderous musings of a German fascist misanthrope.

And yet without a reasonable grasp of Heidegger's thought, there was no way that I could answer the question I had put to myself: "Could an existentialist framework substitute for a positivist one in psychology?"

One weekend when I was dithering about how to confront the Heidegger dilemma, I came upon an article in an old *Partisan Review* on the subject, "What is Existentialism?" William Barrett, one of the editors of the *Review*, was its author.

I had read Barrett's book *Irrational Man*, and it had made a strong impression on me. Moreover, Barrett's *Partisan Review* piece focused directly on Heidegger.

I devoured Barrett's piece, hoping that it might save me from having to read Heidegger for myself. Unfortunately, it didn't do so. But it did succeed in convincing me that Heidegger had directly confronted the issue that I regarded as central to my concern: that Western philosophy early on had adopted a set of premises more suitable for understanding physical objects than human experience.

I suspected that Barrett's piece merely scratched the surface of his knowledge of Heidegger. He was, after all, a distinguished professor of philosophy at New York University as well as an editor of the *Partisan Review*, and he had admitted to having read Heidegger in the original German without having to depend on bad translations.

I hastened to get my hands on a catalog of NYU graduate courses in philosophy and was excited to discover that Barrett was scheduled to give a course on Heidegger the following semester. So I wrote him a letter, requesting permission to audit his course.

I was pleased when he agreed to permit me to do so.

Chapter Thirty-Five

Finding a Better Framework

Once a week in the spring semester of 1964, I found myself taking the subway to attend Professor Barrett's course on Heidegger at NYU. The course gave me the structure and guidance I needed to read Heidegger's *Being and Time* on my own and to get from it what I was looking for.

After absorbing it with the help of Barrett's interpretations, I wasn't at all sure that Heidegger's categories were precisely the right ones for American psychology. But I did feel that he was responsive to the concerns that Whitehead and other philosophers had raised about our philosophical and scientific tradition being more suitable for material objects than for human beings.

For Heidegger, the entire Western tradition in philosophy is off kilter, based on a series of misleading frameworks that Plato and Aristotle introduced in ancient Greece.

Like all frameworks, these are abstractions, illuminating with clarity some aspects of reality while plunging others into obscurity.

Their heritage led ultimately to the invention of the natural sciences— arguably, the supreme and unique achievement of the West. At the same time, however, they built a false base for understanding the human experience.

In Heidegger's view, it was Plato's and Aristotle's answers to certain key philosophical questions that led to our distorted framework for understanding human experience.

Plato and Aristotle were less concerned than Socrates with the existential question of how best to live. They focused instead on the nature of Reality, Truth, and Knowledge. The frameworks that these towering Greek thinkers dreamt up guided the Western philosophy world for the centuries that followed.

For Plato, the true nature of reality is not the everyday world that people experience through their senses (what we see, hear, smell taste, and touch). Instead, for Plato the ability to grasp the true nature of reality belongs solely to the rational intellect. Plato located truth about reality in the mind of the observer.

Following Plato, Aristotle further narrowed what we mean by reality. In his famous work on logic, *The Categories*, Aristotle identified ten ways to describe reality, ways that apply more to objects than to people (e.g., size, shape, location, composition, etc.).

At least in Aristotle's writings, the concept of an object is very broad. Aristotle's world of objects is a world of birth and death: purpose, direction, and fulfillment are possible even for objects like trees. Each object under the sun has its own *potentia*, its opportunities for purposeful growth.

In later centuries, philosophy and science would exclude the purposefulness of objects, narrowing the Aristotelian framework even further.

But what about *human experience* as distinct from objects? What sort of framework or master map would best describe and order the life world of individuals, families, tribes, societies, cultures, civilizations?

The answer, for Heidegger, was clear. Instead of focusing on the features of objects like their quantity, composition, and location, Heidegger focused on how human experience unfolds in *time*.

Time, for Heidegger, is *the* defining characteristic of humanity. We exist, live, and die in time. Plato's master map is timeless and spaceless; Aristotle's is a map of objects occupying space. Heidegger's master map focuses on the temporal dimensions of life.

I was eager to test the credibility of my interpretations by exposing them to the critique of others. So I drafted a paper for a forthcoming meeting of the American Psychological Association, titled "The Impact of Existentialism on Psychology."[1]

I asked Barrett if he would read and critique my draft before I presented the paper. He said he would, and several weeks after I submitted it to him, he asked me if I would have lunch with him. I was pleased with the invitation.

At our lunch in a Greenwich Village bistro, he surprised me by admitting that my presence in his course had caused him some discomfort and a great deal of curiosity. He said that he had been bewildered when he received my request to attend his course, written on my fancy Madison Avenue stationery. (At that time my office was located on Madison Avenue and 56th Street, across the street from IBM's New York headquarters.)

He couldn't understand what conceivable motive an uptown Madison Avenue type, presumably involved with the world of advertising, would have in studying the work of Martin Heidegger. He couldn't see any connection between Heidegger and the selling of soap or cars, he said. It was his curiosity that had persuaded him to grant my request.

He confessed that I had made him uncomfortable by my silence throughout the course. (I had maintained a discreet silence since I didn't want to take time away from the young grad students who were taking the course for credit, and I was also unsure of my ground, having been away from academic philosophy for so many years.)

So, Barrett confessed, he was quite eager to read my paper since he figured it would tell him whether I was for real or some sort of flake who had mistakenly wandered into his course from the Madison Avenue wasteland.

He said that he had actually learned a lot about psychology from my paper—a field with which he was unfamiliar. And he thought I had applied Heidegger's concepts in a novel and interesting fashion. I appreciated Barrett's bemused account of how I had inadvertently succeeded in bewildering him. I had no idea that he was aware of my existence.

Barrett and I eventually became close friends and collaborators, and remained so up to the time of his death many years later.

One of philosophy's most useful aspects is its focus on frameworks—the maps that all disciplines develop to help them think about their specialized slices of reality. The oceanographer brings a different framework to his subject than the poet or the economist. Frameworks are marvelously varied and almost never explicitly recognized, either by believers or by bystanders.

At first glance, the wrong-map problem might seem of concern mainly to specialists in fields such as psychology and economics. But the errors traceable to wrong maps have consequences that extend far beyond these areas of specialization. Our individual well-being, as well as the health and vitality of our culture and the future of our economy, are at stake.

My encounter with Heidegger had convinced me that it was possible to develop frameworks more suitable to human problems than to material objects. My experience with Quine had convinced me that logic, far from being a master key for understanding reality, led instead up a blind alley.

I had learned a lot from my revisit to existentialism.

Chapter Thirty-Six

Applying Philosophy to Psychoanalysis

At some point, I realized that I had overlooked an almost perfect illustration of the wrong-map problem: the then-popular field of psychoanalysis.

Psychoanalysis was a far richer and deeper subject than behaviorism or other branches of psychology. Moreover, it had saddled itself with a massively wrong framework for reasons unrelated to its mission or to its therapeutic practice. And its theoretical foundations were not getting the attention they deserved.

Because of their wrong-map problem, psychoanalysts are obliged to navigate uncomfortably between two strikingly different frameworks. The first is an empirical one—its clinical theory—derived from therapeutic practice. The other is a strange, clumsy set of metaphysical assertions created in the wake of Freud's medical school training in physiology.

The day-to-day practice of psychoanalysis is the source of the first framework. These human interactions have yielded a database unique in human history. The clinical theory is grounded in the everyday life experiences of a vast number of patients. Its raw materials are the patient's hopes and ambitions, fears, fantasies, shifts in mood, outbursts of anger, plus dreams with their wealth of disguised symbols (where a cigar is almost never "just a cigar").

Freud brought to the task of patient treatment an unrelenting willingness to go wherever the facts took him. Thus, the clinical framework of psychoanalysis is relatively easy to understand.

The other framework is much more difficult to understand or use. Freud called it his "metapsychology," as outlined in his *Project for a Scientific Psychology* (1895).

Freud's fondest dream—the heart and soul of his ambition—was to have psychoanalysis recognized as a serious science. Such recognition and acceptance would mean that psychoanalysis had truly reached its full potential. Freud dedicated himself to this goal without reservation.

He developed his more abstract framework because he felt he needed a theory that was more formal and scientific than the one based solely on his clinical experience. As a physiology student, he studied the body's organs: the liver, the heart, and so on. He had been trained to observe strict scientific rigor in these studies.

So he felt uncomfortable with the nonscientific status of his patients' case histories.

Indeed, he referred to them as his "short stories." They may have been interesting, dramatic, and revealing. But they weren't sufficiently scientific, and that demeaned their status in his eyes. Only a formal scientific theory would satisfy his yearnings and ambitions.

His formal medical training had led Freud to come under the influence of the "Helmholtz School," named after its leading representative, a prominent German physiologist who had initially been trained as a physicist.

Helmholtz had made a personal commitment to give physiology a solid foundation in the basic principles of Newtonian physics, in particular the principle of conservation of energy.

This principle is the law of physics developed by James Prescott Joule in 1843, using a descending weight attached to a string that causes a paddle immersed in water to rotate. Joule showed that the gravitational potential energy lost by the weight in descending was equal to the internal heat energy gained by the water through friction with the paddle.

This ingenious experiment showed that energy in this kind of closed system cannot be created or destroyed, but only changed.

Freud swallowed this credo without qualification or hesitation. He immediately launched an ambitious project of forcing his insights about the human condition into a theory based on the principle of heat transfer.

He began his final work, his *Outline of Psychoanalysis*, with this summary statement: "Psychoanalysis makes a basic assumption [the nature of the psychic apparatus], the discussion of which is *reserved to philosophical thought*" (emphasis added).[1]

Freud is acknowledging here that he borrowed his concept of the "psychic apparatus" from philosophy to use as his scientific framework for his clinical observations.

In the psychic apparatus, the instinctual energies of the individual are organized into three systems (ego, id, superego). These energies build up pressures similar to heated water, sometimes generating fierce internal cross-pressures. The energies are discharged in keeping with the principle of conservation of energy, transferred from system to system. Units of this energy (called *cathexes* by Freud) are the basic building blocks that create intrapsychic conflict.

The *psychic apparatus* is clearly a Newtonian mechanism. The philosophical thought to which Freud refers in the quote above is the positivism of his Helmholtz School mentors.

Whitehead called this kind of thought "scientific materialism." This is the doctrine that depicts nature as composed of unrelated bits of matter. There is no meaning to any of it, no larger pattern, no inner coherence. This was the dismal metaphysical underpinning of science that dominated Freud's era. A bleaker worldview would be hard to imagine.

In his therapist role, Freud provided us with a startlingly original picture of human reality. But as an ardent disciple of the Helmholtz School, he still had to please his old professors whose authoritarian principles he had internalized. So he laboriously converted his highly original observations of patients into the positivist framework of his teachers, thereby confusing the hell out of generations of therapists who followed in his footsteps.

As late as 1929, thirty-four years after drafting his *Project for a Scientific Psychology*, Freud was still writing that the human organism is to be conceived of as a system of small particles moved by two forces according to the principle of the conservation of energy. The forces are the same two forces found in physical nature: attraction and repulsion. In their application to human psychology, Freud came to call these forces the *life instinct* and the *death instinct*.

Ironically, he never subjected his *scientific* psychology to the same strict standard of observation and critique as he did his *clinical* psychology. He was *himself* thus pulled in two opposing directions. As a physician, his ethical commitment to help his patients led him into an intense human encounter with them. As a scientist, his commitment led him in the opposite direction. He felt obliged to translate these human encounters into what he falsely considered to be the language and concepts of science.

Though a great thinker and a superb observer, Freud's efforts to explain his patients' problems in terms of Newtonian science often come close to nonsense. People are not water boilers building up sexual and aggressive instinctual pressures as if they were heads of steam. The human psyche is not a mechanical apparatus constantly seeking to rid itself of stimulation. It is not illuminating to explain human behavior by reducing it to quanta of libidinal energies. The human person is simply not best understood as a Newtonian mechanism obeying the laws of classical physics.

Constantly, for nearly a half century, Freud fussed with his clinical theory in order to make it more scientific. Paradoxically, he ended up doing the exact opposite of what he had intended. Instead of *enhancing* the scientific status of psychoanalysis, he actually put up *barriers* to its advancement.

Suppose that instead of lavishing so much effort in constructing a picture of the human psyche as a boiler-like edifice, Freud had instead simply insisted that psychoanalysts describe and document their successes and failures in dealing with each patient's symptoms. This would have allowed the therapists to assess psychological symptoms in a replicable way, and then to test the interventions that seemed to work best.

If only Freud had held a simpler, more practical conception of science, psychoanalysis might have enjoyed a different—and better—fate.

In recent years, the status of psychoanalysis has steadily lost ground. At the present time, psychoanalytic influence has virtually disappeared from departments of psychiatry in medical schools and is often treated as a relic in academic departments of psychology.

Yet Freud's core concepts have been so thoroughly absorbed into the culture that they are taken for granted. Most forms of psychological therapy are grounded in basic psychoanalytic concepts, whether acknowledged or not. Freud's discoveries about unconscious motivation are an important part of our intellectual heritage, but psychoanalytic theory has been rejected as serious science.

Freud admitted that his patients confirmed for him that the core values of work and love give meaning to life. Though he was not conventionally religious, in conversation with the existential psychiatrist Ludwig Binswanger, he assigned the highest value to *Geist* (spirit). Binswanger writes, "I could hardly believe my ears when I heard Freud say, 'Yes, *Geist* is everything.'"[2]

Without values that celebrate the human spirit, therapies are mere technologies. In placing the arid ideologies of the Helmholtz School ahead of his own core life values, Freud made a fatally wrong existential choice.

The more I thought about psychoanalysis, the more convinced I became that it was ideal for my purposes. No other branch of psychology could benefit more from a makeover of its philosophical premises, and conversely, philosophy itself could learn something valuable about the human condition from psychoanalysis.

Chapter Thirty-Seven

"Ego and Instinct" in Retrospect

Psychoanalysis had inadvertently become a battleground for two opposing philosophical worldviews—the worldview of positivism underlying Freud's scientific theory versus the existential worldview underlying its clinical theory and practice. [1]

I knew that it would be useful to extricate psychoanalytic theory from its positivist framework.

Freud had struggled mightily to understand how the forces of reason and unreason play out in the lives of individuals. But the question he had struggled with the most remained open. Are the rational and nonrational aspects of human life pitted against each other in irreconcilable conflict (*Ego versus Instinct*, as Freud argued) or are they complementary aspects of human flourishing?

In conducting research for the book I intended to write, I felt I knew enough to guide my analysis of the psychoanalytic literature. But I wasn't confident that I had a sufficient mastery of the philosophical literature to achieve the book's ambitious goal—to replace Freud's useless and convoluted philosophical framework (his metapsychology) with a framework easier for therapists to manage.

I had come to appreciate William Barrett's grasp of philosophical issues, as expressed in his book *Irrational Man* and other writings. It seemed to me that were he willing to coauthor my book with me, he could help me tease out what psychoanalysts reveals about the nature—and limits—of human reason. Together, I felt, we could examine the conceptual contradictions baked into the foundations of psychoanalysis, and why its outmoded philosophical framework frustrated its efforts to conduct research on its effectiveness as a form of therapy, thereby blocking its path to becoming a viable science.

After mulling it over, I hesitantly invited Barrett to coauthor the book with me. I told him that I was willing to do the heavy lifting on the psychoanalytic side and also do the bulk of the actual writing. I invited him to draft the parts of the philosophy chapters that interested him the most and to edit the parts that I wrote.

His quick and enthusiastic response was encouraging. It assured me that our coauthorship might succeed in clarifying a fascinating philosophical issue that was crippling an important form of psychological therapy.

I think that Barrett and I did a nifty piece of analysis—a clear demonstration of the conflicting philosophical sources of psychoanalysis and the damage that this unresolved conflict inflicted on its theory and practice.

Why, then, is psychoanalysis faring so badly today? The short answer, I think, is that it became accustomed to the absence of research on the effectiveness of its interventions. Even when such research became feasible to conduct, the incentive was lacking and lethargy prevailed.

With its high costs in fees and time without health care insurance coverage, and without constant research-based feedback to improve its effectiveness, it has continued to lose ground as a practical form of therapy. But its influence permeates our culture in countless ways.

Sexual repression is far less prevalent today than in Freud's era. One might expect that our vast increase in freedom of sexual expression would liberate people from the neuroses that large-scale cultural repression creates, making us emotionally freer and healthier.

Ironically, my studies of our culture's changing mores convey the opposite message. Scratch the surface of the lives of most Americans and you will find a rich repository of neurotic problems that diminish freedom of action and quality of life.

Among less affluent Americans, these psychological problems are often overwhelmed by practical problems such as stagnant wages and job loss. But the neuroses of middle-class, upwardly mobile Americans continue to flower in full bloom.

If the definition of neurosis is the experience of being whipped about by forces you do not understand and cannot control, your freedom and autonomy are greatly enhanced when you learn what these forces are. And you can sometimes bring them under some degree of control. The means for doing so include therapy, but also include learning from life and from personal relationships.

My impression is that in today's culture, people's neuroses are more diffuse and less encapsulated than they used to be. People suffering from neurosis have symptoms that are often vague, difficult to define, and shift around a lot. I believe that this reflects the reality that our culture provides less support and direction to individuals about what really matters than it used to.

The ethos of our culture is uncertain and wobbly. It imparts a sense of entitlement that leads to one disappointment after another. It celebrates individual freedom, but undermines community and cohesiveness.

The culture of Freud's day discouraged individual self-expressiveness in the interest of maintaining a stable, highly stratified society. Our current post-Freudian culture could hardly be more different. But in today's culture, the neuroses are thriving to as great an extent, if not greater, than in the past.

To address them, new forms of therapy have proliferated wildly, but much of today's angst is not susceptible to treatment by professionals for a fee.

On the very first page of chapter 1 of *Ego and Instinct*, we recount the following episode:

> A few years ago a well-known public figure in the communications world, whom we shall call Mr. N., ended a long period of depression and emotional turmoil by taking his own life. For several years he had been under the care of a noted psychoanalyst almost as prominent as himself. In the months preceding N's suicide, the psychoanalyst had dropped virtually all of his other responsibilities to place himself at the disposal of his patient and friend.
>
> When N died the psychoanalyst felt a sense of poignant personal loss, much like the grief of the immediate family. Sometime later a colleague of the psychoanalyst, who had also known N, wondered aloud whether his suicide might have been prevented if the psychoanalyst had been a slightly different sort of person. "Don't get me wrong," he said. "In many ways my colleague is a most gifted and unusual psychoanalyst. Certainly, he's a lot smarter than I am. But I wonder whether I might have been able to save N if *I* had taken care of him."
>
> He went on to explain: "My colleague is a brilliant man and a thorough intellectual. So, of course, was N. They locked themselves indoors for hours on end, analyzing, analyzing, analyzing. Maybe, just maybe if I had taken N outside of that damned library and walked with him . . . long walks through the countryside . . . " His voice trailed off. After a long pause he added: "I'm a more physical type, more down to earth. Maybe if it had all been a little simpler and more basic—less intellectual—N might have shaken himself out of it."[2]

The second psychoanalyst, the one who thought that a less intellectual approach might have saved N, is undoubtedly oversimplifying the situation. Long walks are unlikely to alleviate serious depressions.

But we felt that this therapist, however overoptimistic, was groping toward a point that we deemed essential.

Fee-for-service professional therapy (however skillful) is poorly designed to cope with existential despair, anxiety, confusion, and bewilderment.

That is why we put this true story at the very beginning of our book. It announced its central theme: *Psychological therapy is not itself the decisive force in self-transformation. It can only remove neurotic obstacles and provide the client/patient with a sympathetic ear during the transition from one phase of life to another.*

Psychological therapies, including psychoanalysis, do not often, if ever, lead to existential and religious sorts of self-transformation.

Neurotic anxiety most often has its roots in connections established in childhood. *Existential* anxiety is an experience that can—and does—occur at any age or stage of life: the experience of confronting the strangeness of the world and not feeling at home in it.

We do not celebrate writers like Kafka, Camus, and Kierkegaard for their neuroses, but for the eloquent ways in which they expressed their existential quest for meaning in a world that they experienced as strange and alien.

Neurotic anxiety and spiritual anguish may overlap, but they are decidedly different states of being. Psychological therapies can help with the neurotic aspects of life, but other paths beckon those whose struggles are of a spiritual existential nature.

Many people have undergone existential self-transformation. It can come in a variety of forms—with love, with certain kinds of intimate friendship, with near-death experience, with a religious epiphany, with hitting bottom, with finding something larger to connect to, with new life commitments.

Psychological therapy to liberate one from the dismal prison of neurotic anxiety sometimes can open that path.

Chapter Thirty-Eight

The Mind-set of the Iron Cage: Prying It Open

In June 1982, the Aspen Institute held a meeting in Berlin to honor Germany's intellectual heritage.

As a member of the institute, I was invited to prepare a lecture for the occasion. The institute's motto is "thought leading to action." My lecture was to focus on how German philosophical thought might lead to action on the challenges facing the Western democracies.

I accepted the invitation with relish. Most of my speaking invitations focused on my public opinion research. I welcomed this rare opportunity to discuss a set of issues that had been nagging at me for years.

Since my lecture took place in Berlin, I wanted to share with the audience why I felt that certain strands of German philosophy could be particularly useful to our thinking about issues in the United States as well as in Germany.

One such strand was the philosophical tool the Germans call "critique." In our American usage, the word *critique* has such a broad range of meanings that it is almost meaningless. But in German thought, critique has a specific history, meaning, and methodology.

The main objective of critique is to uncover sources of distortion and crooked thinking in people's frameworks, especially distortions that may not be fully conscious and that therefore need a special tool to expose them.

Philosopher Karl Polanyi coined the term *tacit knowledge* to refer to our culture's implicit and mostly unconscious sense of reality about the world. All of us absorb the frameworks dominant in the broader culture, or in the subcultures to which we belong.

The tacit knowledge that shapes our frameworks dominates our thought processes to a greater extent than most people realize. *Making these tacit*

165

frameworks explicit, subjecting them to rigorous examination (critique), and adapting them to changing conditions became one of my ideals of genuine philosophical work.

Kant was the first modern German philosopher who used the tool of critique to uncover distortions in Germany philosophy. Following Kant, an impressive tradition of German thinkers applied the technique of critique in a compelling fashion.

I was particularly interested in how two outstanding German thinkers—Max Weber in the nineteenth and early twentieth centuries and Jurgen Habermas, born in 1929 and still alive—applied the practice of critique. They extended their critiques to uncover major distortions in Western frameworks of thought.

Weber developed a masterful critique of these distortions. In Weber's view, an intellectual ideology he called "instrumental rationality" had become the dominant way of thinking in the West and was distorting every aspect of the culture of his time.

Instrumental rationality is our tendency to rob life of its subjectivity and inwardness and to look for a technological fix for every problem. This mentality has brutally twisted the *lebenswelt* out of shape—the everyday world of human bonds, beliefs, feelings, love, work, loyalty, morality, politics, family relations, and friendship.

In the lecture, I summarized Weber's critique as follows:

> Weber saw the growth of instrumental rationality as the master key to our history. His great fear was that its power would ultimately destroy the quality of western civilization.
>
> At one point he described its effects as "an icy cold polar night." He predicted that it would shape the social character of twentieth-century humanity so adversely that the typical individual would be "a heartless expert."
>
> In his most familiar metaphor, he described this mind-set as an "iron cage" imprisoning the human spirit and cutting us off from the deepest sources of our being. This iron cage strips life of all mystery and charm, destroying what the English philosopher Edmund Burke called the "inns and resting places of the human spirit."[1]

I went on to note that the contemporary German philosopher Jurgen Habermas had further elaborated Weber's theme. For Habermas, the objective of science (and of instrumental rationality) had been to *dominate* nature. But the objective of everyday social/political life is not, he urged, to dominate everything and everyone.

When large groups of people live together, we encounter questions such as: how do we keep from dominating and destroying each other? How do we reinforce the human bonds that hold society together?

Clearly, techniques designed for domination and control are not sound methods for finding answers to these questions. Instead, we need new methods that are not coercive.

Habermas labels such noncoercive methods as "communicative action." They apply only in settings in which all traces of manipulation and domination have been eliminated.

In my lecture I concluded, "The thrust of Habermas's thought is not so much to destroy the iron cage formed by instrumental rationality as to pry it open a bit—to break its hold on our conception of rationality. The sphere of the rational is expanded to encompass the domain of meanings, feelings, speech, and other forms of understanding human relationships."

Applying critique to policy thinkers in the United States, I went on to say that our American worldviews (*Weltanschauung*) were "imprisoned within frameworks of thought that harbor outmoded philosophies from other eras."

Experiences such as the meeting at Bilderberg had persuaded me that many elite American policy makers are convinced in advance that all issues are fundamentally matters either of money or power. This conviction leads them either to throw money at problems or to regard legislation, regulation, and military force as the preferred solution to policy problems.

This strategy may work well enough for the many problems that *do* involve money or power. But they don't work well for problems that are mainly cultural.

I said,

> The central feature of most American elite worldviews is how they conceive reality. . . . What weight should one give to industrial strength? Or financial stability? How important are treaties or ties with allies? How important are moral considerations? What weight should be given to cultural matters? How important is diplomacy? How much influence should be assigned to leadership?
>
> Unfortunately, many policy makers do not reserve judgment about the relative importance of the various forces. They bring their value judgments with them *before* they ever encounter the issue. They do not say, "In this instance, military power counts; in that instance, let's forget about the balance of power and try to reach a better mutual understanding of each other's problems."
>
> To a startling degree, our leaders transform the large political and moral dilemmas of our time into technical issues. This renders them inaccessible to public understanding and judgment. It effectively excludes the bulk of the citizenry from influencing policy. It is as if the "experts" were a class apart, sharing a rarified culture and a pool of knowledge the uninitiated could not possibly grasp.

> Translating ethical issues into technical ones is so much a part of the contemporary zeitgeist that is difficult for us to comprehend how arbitrary and one-sided it is.

Once you begin to focus on strategies for changing *culture*, your frame of reference needs to shift away from an exclusive concern with money, power, and regulation to arrive at radically different forms of intervention. For example, a strategy without stringent regulation may be bad for the economy, but it has proven a sensible and realistic strategy for *changing cultural norms*.

In recent decades our society has witnessed vast amounts of cultural change. Not that long ago, middle-class men were the exclusive breadwinners in their families. The male as a "good provider" was a standard feature of our culture. Other standard cultural norms included strict childhood discipline, a certain prudery, cigarette smoking after sex, and in-the-closet status for gays.

These cultural habits were taken for granted and almost universal. Now these aspects of our culture have changed almost beyond recognition.

Our society has much more control over its own fate than most of us presuppose. To exercise it, however, we need to redefine and redescribe many of our problems as cultural in nature rather than as technical issues of economics or balance of power.

Automatically giving priority to hard power over soft power, automatically converting value issues into technical ones, automatically assuming that expert knowledge and insights are vastly superior to public ways of knowing—these elite habits of mind and worldviews are deeply rooted in the Western tradition.

The critiques of Max Weber and Jurgen Habermas still have relevance today. I see "instrumental rationality" everywhere I look, and I believe we would be well served if we were to adopt Habermas's methods of "communicative action"—but give it better name.

In particular, I believe that our prejudice that money and power constitute reality has crippled our pragmatic problem-solving abilities.

We have ignored culture as the main source of many of our most serious problems, and consequently have scanted our efforts to learn how to change cultural values as a key source of action.

Chapter Thirty-Nine

Don't Fight Human Nature!

A philosophy of life that ignored human nature inevitably would be unstable and flimsy, ready to fall apart at the first sign of stress. This reality may seem self-evident. But, in fact, surprisingly few such robust theories exist.

In my intellectually formative years, leading thinkers were hostile to the idea of human nature. This is because they associated it with obsolete reactionary ideologies.

Most of them linked the concept of human nature with religious dogma of the past: dogma that justified the divine rights of kings, slavery, the subordination of secular society to religious authority, the subordination of women, and static societies mired in poverty and rigid class systems.

The social thinkers of my youth drew their inspiration from the modern secular tradition. They were strong advocates of the Enlightenment's celebration of human rationality and the ability of the human person to shape his or her own life.

The dominant academic assumption throughout most of my life was that the human mind was a "tabula rasa"—a blank slate on which human experience could write its own story.[1] This notion of the human psyche as a blank slate is deeply embedded in the doctrines of Western civilization that have led to democracy and political freedom.

Small wonder that social thinkers embraced it, rather than endorsing a theory of human nature tied to prescientific religious authoritarianism and class-ridden political regimes.

But the blank slate theory is far from a harmless idea. It is responsible for many political failures and deaths. In the hands of semimaniacal Communist leaders like Josef Stalin, Pol Pot, and Mao Tse Tung, the idea that humans can be transformed to fit like cogs into a preconceived conception of an idealized society has led to the slaughter of millions of people.

169

The theory of human nature I have come to embrace runs directly counter to the theory of the blank state. It emphasizes the *nonrational, nonconscious* aspects of the human condition.

Contemporary neuroscience has reinforced my conviction that most of our thinking is unconscious and that we are largely unaware of our deepest assumptions. It is these assumptions rather than facts, logic, and rational thinking that dominate our decision making.

The main obstacle to understanding human nature is that one never encounters it in pure form, unaffected by nurture. Even in the womb, experience and culture influence and shape who we are and how we behave. Nature and nurture are inextricably linked.

Controversy about the relative dominance of inborn human traits runs through the history of Western civilization. For centuries social thinkers have engaged in endless arguments about the nature/nurture issue and how much weight to assign to each.

The most simple and concrete way to identify human nature may be through ethnography. Since there are so many cultures in the world, and since they vary so greatly, one can ask: "Are there any human traits that are *universal to all cultures*—from the most 'primitive' to the most 'advanced,' from the most isolated to the ones most enmeshed in external influences?"

Ethnographer Donald E. Brown published a list of such traits in 1991.[2] I find Brown's list of universal traits valuable for several reasons. It has such immense breadth that it makes the concept of a blank slate seem blind to reality.

To absorb the full range of our communality as humans is to begin to understand the importance of human nature. Brown's enumeration makes the idea of human nature concrete and brings it down to earth.

A sampling from Brown's list of things that one universally finds evidence of in all cultures is below.

This sampling constitutes less than 20 percent of Brown's list. But it is broad enough to give us a concrete sense that many of the traits we ordinarily associate with human nature are indeed part and parcel of the human condition across all cultures.

Baby talk	Gossip	Nepotism
Beliefs about death and religion	Government	Play
Beliefs about fortune and misfortune	Hairstyles	Poetry
Body adornments	Hope	Prestige inequality
Collective identities	Hospitality	Pride

Copulation conducted in privacy	Incest taboo	Property
Coyness displays	Jokes	Proverbs
Customary greetings	Judging others	Rites of passage
Dance	Law	Self as responsible agent
Death rituals	Magic	Sexuality as a source of jealousy
Distinguishing between right and wrong	Males dominate public sphere	Shame
Dream interpretation	Marriage	Statuses and roles
Envy	Meal times	Thumb sucking
Ethnocentrism	Moral sentiment	Tickling
Facial expression of disgust, fear, sadness, joy	Mourning	Tools to make tools
Fairness	Murder proscribed	True and false distinguished
Fasting	Music	Visiting
Gift giving	Myths	

Chapter Forty

Co-evolution

The evidence from ethnography gives us bountiful examples of universal human traits. But it doesn't help us to understand the dynamics of how human nature is formed and how it evolves.

For that understanding we need to look to other branches of science, and to a doctrine sometimes referred to as "co-evolution." This doctrine assumes that evolution takes place simultaneously at three levels—genetically, culturally, and through individual maturation.

The mechanisms for each of the three processes are vastly different.

Dr. George Vaillant, longtime director of Harvard's Study of Adult Development, puts the doctrine of co-evolution in a useful time frame. He writes that over a period of more than two hundred million years, "walnut-sized brained, untrusting, humorless, cold-blooded reptiles slowly evolved into warm-blooded, child-nurturing . . . large-brained mammals."[1] *Genetic* evolution takes place on a time scale measured in terms of hundreds of millions of years.

On the other hand, our *cultural* evolution as humans has occurred over a tiny fraction of that time—approximately one-tenth of 1 percent. As Vaillant describes it, "Then, abruptly, less than 200,000 years ago, a new subspecies, *Homo sapiens sapiens,* from whom all human beings are descended, evolved in what is now Kenya and Ethiopia."[2]

Not long thereafter (about 150,000 years ago) language appeared, vastly accelerating human development. With language, knowledge could be handed down to children and to others in the tribe, giving the cultural development of *Homo sapiens* a decisive evolutionary advantage over the Neanderthal branch of humanity.

In the third form of evolution, *individual maturation*, the time scale once again dramatically shifts downward—to the span of a single lifetime. Even with mere decades of experience, individuals can learn to transcend the limits of their culture as well as the immaturity of their younger years. Sometimes they even achieve a degree of spiritual maturation.

Vaillant's research project—the Harvard Study of Adult Development—tracks the lives of several hundred Harvard men over a period of more than sixty years. It is the world's longest longitudinal study. The research team began to study their subjects' styles of managing their lives while they were sophomores at Harvard, in the years just prior to WWII.

They followed up with each of their subjects annually, carefully analyzing how their lives developed as they aged through their twenties, thirties, forties, fifties, sixties, and seventies. In analyzing the full span of adult maturation, Vaillant applied to these Harvard men a modified version of Erik Erikson's theory of human development.

Erikson describes human development as a series of stages, each with its own distinctive life task: developing basic trust as a child; establishing a sense of identity as an adolescent; achieving intimacy in personal relationships, consolidating one's own lifestyle, and caring for others as an adult; and representing the meaning of one's life experience as an older person.

Most of us pursue these tasks in a fairly orderly sequence, but they can also be skipped or addressed out of sequence.

The signs of our biologically endowed human nature are present in every stage. We are constantly busy with the genetically based human tasks of mating; nurturing and being nurtured; grooming; preening; competing *and* cooperating for access to resources; being self-expressive and creative; struggling for status, security, stability, and acceptance.

In an ever-changing environment, it would be convenient if we could modify our genetic structure to adapt to new circumstances. But we cannot change our genome at will. (Not yet, at least.) The time scale of genetic change is simply too vast. Culture is another matter. Culture is indispensable to shaping our lives, and it *is* subject to change.

Culture is indispensable to human development and it pervades every stage of our lives. A prime example of our dependence on culture is the maternal care of children. The human infant is full of amazing potential and yet is radically incomplete when born. Babies achieve normal development thanks primarily to the nurturing attention of the maternal parent.

The culture dictates the forms of child care that mothers provide for their children, especially during the baby's first high-risk years.

If human flourishing depends critically on our culture being evolution-friendly, the key question becomes: how evolution-friendly is it? Does our culture support sufficiently prolonged nurturing for the babies born into it? Does it provide adults with enough (and the right sorts) of mating/parenting opportunities? Are our cultural norms and values consonant with what we know about human sexuality? Do they provide at least a minimum degree of stability and social cohesiveness? Are there opportunities for expressiveness in the form of art, rituals, religion? Does the culture regulate behavior sufficiently to keep violence, criminality, and injustice within tolerable bounds?

The requirement of being evolution-friendly gives culture great strategic importance in assuring human flourishing. Without the guidance of culture, individual behavior would flounder and all of us would be trapped in the random destructiveness of people driven by conflicts between their own primitive inborn desires and those of others.

The vivid contrast among the three radically different time scales dramatizes the point that human development is truly a work in progress. Humans could not survive, let alone thrive, on genes alone. Our biological makeup and our big brains provide us with the flexibility and smarts to survive and flourish—provided that our culture guides us in the right direction.

Several other branches of science enrich this co-evolutionary perspective. Neuroscience in particular highlights the picture of humans as essentially *nonrational creatures of emotion.*

Our Western intellectual tradition favors rationality and disapproves of the nonrational. Indeed, this disapproval is so pervasive that we find it difficult to conceive of the nonrational in positive ways.

Consider, for example, our conception of "good judgment." We tend to assume that people with good judgment are not swayed by their emotions, and that strong emotions lead to bad judgment. Sound judgment, it is assumed, is based on rational considerations free of the distorting influence of emotion.

Recent findings suggest, however, that this dichotomy between reason and emotion is all wrong. Antonio Damascio and other neuroscientists have accumulated evidence that the nonrational emotions are an inherent, necessary part of the brain's judgment-making processes.

Cognitive psychology is another branch of science that enriches our understanding of the nonrational aspects life.

Two outstanding cognitive psychologists, Daniel Kahneman and Adam Twersky, made a systematic effort to overthrow "the dogmatic assumption that the human mind is rational and logical." They set out to demonstrate that "our minds are susceptible to systemic error" and that people are led astray not by their emotions but by the inherent "design of the machinery of cognition."[3]

Over a ten-year period, the two psychologists published two important articles: the first on judgment errors; the second on a theory of decision making they called "prospect theory."

This second article is a pillar of the discipline of behavioral economics and the basis for Kahneman's Nobel Prize in economics in 2002. (The fact that Kahneman, a psychologist, received a Nobel prize in *economics* is revealing. No field more desperately needs a realistic theory of human nature than does economics.)

In 2011 Kahneman published his masterpiece, *Thinking, Fast and Slow*. In it, he states that its purpose is to "improve our ability to identify and understand errors of judgment and choice [and] to limit the damage that bad judgments and choices often cause."[4]

The thesis of the book is that we are inherently error-prone creatures who cling passionately to our biases and errors of judgment despite the marvels of our thinking processes.

Over a period of decades, Kahneman conducted a series of experiments to identify the automatic and unconscious processes of our everyday thinking. His cognitive experiments led him to conclude that our minds have multiple inherent tendencies to distort reality.

Kahneman concluded that our minds automatically distort reality in a number of important ways. We tend to

- leap to unwarranted conclusions;
- impose an artificial narrative coherence on events;
- suspend disbelief, skepticism, and uncertainty that may be fully warranted;
- falsely attribute causality to random or loosely correlated events and happenings;
- prove excessively gullible and optimistically establish strong patterns of unrealistic expectations;
- apply the halo effect indiscriminately;
- resort automatically to stereotypes and heuristics; and
- possess a characteristic Kahneman calls WYSIATI, an acronym that stands for the phrase "what you see is all there is." We tend to ignore virtually all realities and considerations that are not present at the time of judgment.

The one common element to the scientific findings of evolutionary biology, cognitive psychology, and neuroscience is the view of human nature as *non*rational.

This emphatically does not mean *irrational* in the sense of crazy or abnormal. It simply means that it is inaccurate to conceive of humans as rational beings who think, act, and live in the kind of calculated, self-interested ways that the most faithful adherents of the Enlightenment tradition think they do.

The truth is that people often do not know what their self-interest is.

Rarely do they understand the emotions that drive them and the assumptions underlying their own belief systems. Much of the time we humans don't know what is going on in our own psyches: our mental and emotional life is largely unconscious. Our self-protective defenses often backfire, almost in the same way that a person's immune system can backfire and turn his own body against him.

In brief, the findings of recent science suggest a quite robust theory of human nature. Each and every individual on earth is the product of an incredibly complex process of coordination among three radically different systems.

The first is our genetic evolution. Deep down, we remain creatures of inborn primitive responses and emotions over which we have little control.

The second system is our cultural evolution over which we have some degree of control (and are learning to gain more). Without the guidance of culture, we wouldn't be able to build stable societies and civilizations.

The third system is individual thought, learning, and development that unfolds in stages. We have considerable control over this aspect of evolution, which we exercise though highly imperfect mechanisms of cognition and adaptation.

Chapter Forty-One

Culture Is Inescapable . . .

We are all dependent on culture. Life is too short to rely exclusively on individual experience to guide decision making on the important issues of living. We all know that one learns from one's own mistakes. The hope, of course, is that having learned from our mistakes, we then go on to live better lives.

But suppose we discover that it's too late to repair the damage? I've had that disheartening experience more than once. Any one life is too short and too chopped up to provide a manual on how to correct one's mistakes in a timely fashion.

Our paltry eight or so decades of life is trivial compared to the tens of thousands of years of communal life embodied in culture. The role of human culture is to be the repository of the cumulative wisdom that people have acquired since the advent of language about 150 millennia ago. We must look to culture for guidance on how to survive and flourish, and to learn what really matters. That is its evolutionary role.

We are constantly busy with the developmental tasks of growing up, raising a family, making a living, and seeking to insure a comfortable retirement. We don't have enough time on this earth to benefit fully from personal experience. So we depend on culture.

But our dependence is invariably difficult. This is because all cultures have weird, dysfunctional features. Islamic culture dictates that wives thought guilty of adultery be stoned to death (in 2013 there were more than nine hundred such stonings in Pakistan). African culture subjects young girls to genital cutting. Indian culture puts wives who bring an insufficient dowry into their marriage at risk of serious abuse. American culture still discriminates against men and women based on race and ethnicity.

There are many reasons why cultures become quirky and dysfunctional. Co-evolution calls for such a staggering degree of coordination between the forces of nature and nurture that it is a miracle that human culture with all its flaws functions as well as it does.

Cultures achieve the goal of being evolution-friendly through a series of fragile balancing acts for the conflicting desires of our nature. They are fragile because they elude our conscious control. We take them for granted until they break down, at which point the culture is plunged into turmoil.

Until recently, our American culture supported many of the positive balances needed for both the culture and individuals to flourish.

- The high cultural value we placed on equality of opportunity permitted us to maintain a realistic balance between equality and freedom.
- We mostly succeeded in balancing the imperatives of a free enterprise economy and meeting the needs of our most vulnerable citizens.
- We achieved a good balance between almost-full employment and a flexible labor market.
- Our culture supported our citizens who hold strong religious beliefs, while at the same time guaranteeing freedom of religion.
- Our culture encouraged sexual self-expression and single-parent families at the same time that it encouraged stable family life.

Achieving the right set of balances takes trial and error. Trial and error takes time, lots of it. Cultural experimentation can consume several lifetimes before a sound nurture/nature balance in any one area becomes incorporated into our cultural norms.

For example, in recent decades our cultural norms on marriage have grown less restrictive. There is far less stigma attached to marital breakup than in the past. Individual freedom is important to human flourishing. But so is the stability that comes from the restraints on freedom in marriage.

At the present time, the cultural scales are tipped in favor of freedom. It may take several more generations before our culture discovers the optimum balance in marriage between individual freedom and stable commitment—at the cost of generations of broken lives.

My firm and I were able to document the many imbalances that arose in the wake of America's cultural revolution. Here are five of the most consequential imbalances.

"EXPRESSIVE INDIVIDUALISM" THREATENS TO OVERWHELM AMERICAN CULTURE.

The college student forerunners of our cultural revolution put equal emphasis on individual freedom and communal life. But as the cultural revolution evolved, the demand for individual freedom intensified while communal values eroded.

I refer to this trend as "expressive individualism."

The core conviction of the cultural revolution was that America had become so affluent that sacrifice of the expressive side of life was no longer an economic imperative. We could have both economic well-being *and* freedom to express our true selves.

Between the mid-1970s and mid-1980s, expressive individualism began to dominate the culture. As it grew ever stronger, it came to threaten the delicate balance between individual desires and the well-being of the larger culture.

When expressive individualism becomes excessive, it reaches a tipping point where lack of concern with the larger community poses a threat to our future well-being.

EQUATING WHAT IS RIGHT WITH WHAT IS LEGAL UNDERMINES OUR SOCIAL ETHOS.

Like the majority of Americans, I had welcomed the opportunity to escape the rigid conformity of the 1950s. But I have been appalled by one of its consequences: the equating of right and wrong with legal and illegal. I grew up with the belief that right and wrong are independent of legality. You can do great harm and still remain within the limits of the law.

For societies and free market economies to flourish, they need a sturdy ethical layer superimposed atop the legal system. The legal system guarantees some degree of stability and justice. The ethical overlay elevates the economy and the society from mere stability to the status of a genuine community.

People in positions of power in our economy have learned to rationalize egregious behavior by falling back on the self-exonerating excuse "I didn't do anything wrong. I didn't break the law. Everything we did was legal." In many groups, there is an unspoken agreement that "It's okay to game the system."

Defining ethics in terms of legality has contributed to the vacuum of moral standards that sociologists label "anomie." It is a terrible thing for a society to lose its ethical centeredness.

GROUPTHINK AND A TRIBAL MENTALITY EXACERBATE OUR NATION'S PROBLEMS.

My work has made me aware that people in organizations and groups often echo one another rather than express independent views. They keep repeating the same phrases often in the same tone of voice.

If I had been exposed to only a few groups, I might not have been as struck by the repetitious and ritualistic qualities of tribal-like groupthink. But my work in public opinion brings me into contact with groups from a wide variety of subcultures, ranging from university trustees and business boards of directors to trade union leaders, judges, teachers, investors, beer drinkers, voters, antiwar protesters, city council members, alcoholics, chambers of commerce, foreign policy elites, feminists, antiabortion activists, steel workers, and community college dropouts.

Sometimes meetings with these various groups assume an almost primitive quality, and I have felt as if I were invited to participate in tribal confabs without actually being a member of the tribe.

I have learned to mistrust the pronouncements and judgments that come from such meetings. The tribal mentality, as I have encountered it, serves the purpose of forging its members into a cohesive group. It would have been naïve to expect independent thought and objective judgment from these rituals.

This sort of tribal groupthink is a major source of untruths and distortions in American life today. (For example, the conviction among economists that markets are self-correcting mechanisms.) Tribal mentality is so widespread, so universal, so comforting for the group and so lacking in objectivity that it becomes a major force in creating self-deception.

I developed great respect for those organizations willing to tear down the veil of groupthink and accept critical judgments on their past performance.

OUR ELITES SEEM CLUELESS IN SHAPING SOUND PUBLIC JUDGMENT.

It is, I believe, the responsibility of the nation's elites, especially in the media, to guide public opinion away from thoughtless "raw opinion" toward genuine public judgment. At the very least, our institutions should not short-circuit the process.

Unfortunately, elites in our leading institutions do not accept this responsibility. They often take the public's ignorance and inattention as an opportunity to manipulate public policy.

Indeed, the media inadvertently undermine the core principles of democracy they so passionately preach. For example, in order to let viewers make up their own minds on issues, public television ritualistically presents opposing experts in debate format. Each expert is given equal time. Each expert typically states views diametrically opposed to the other. These debates are often burdened with technical jargon. They can leave viewers even more confused than they had been (for example, the televised debates on climate change).

The media also exaggerate the relevance of factual information in helping the public reach judgment on an issue. The public is not an information-processing machine. People judge issues primarily on how they fit into their value system.

FLAWED FRAMEWORKS LEAD OUR PROFESSIONS ASTRAY.

The philosophical frameworks of experts often get in the way of the public's understanding of issues. This is especially true of economic issues. All too often, the views of economic experts have little to do with empirical observations of how markets actually work (the presumed basis of economic science).

Instead, their opinions have everything to do with assumptions about human behavior and the nature of markets. These assumptions are built into the philosophical framework of the majority of American economists.

In one of his most quoted observations, John Maynard Keynes commented that those who believe that their thinking is not influenced by philosophy are usually, in fact, the victims of some "defunct metaphysician."

Keynes's observation applies to all the social sciences. Each discipline favors its own area of specialization.

- Economists overweight economic factors. Economists believe they are being scientific when they express their theories mathematically without troubling to verify how well their mathematical models work in the actual world.
- Sociologists ignore most aspects of social reality in favor of social structure and norms. Many academic departments of sociology are floundering for lack of a clear objective or method.
- Psychologists favor psychological factors.
- Political scientists focus on transient power realities. Political science has grown too highly specialized to test broad political theories.
- Students of the natural sciences emphasize the building blocks of nature—elementary particles, atoms, cells, genes, strings, strands of DNA, and how they interact. The implications for the world outside science are left to work themselves out.[1]

The creativity of human experience lies as much in patterns of connected-ness as in isolated elements. When you focus on the *connections* rather than on the raw materials, you are mapping a radically different aspect of being.

At some critical point in the process of connectivity, something new under the sun is created, including life itself. Freud and his followers failed to pinpoint *connectivity*, both within and outside the self, as the psyche's core process—often positive, as in mother-baby connections that build basic trust in the infant, but sometimes negative, as in the failures of connectedness between mother and infant that result in lifelong problems with intimacy.

Our democracy has been around for almost two and a half centuries. One would have thought that by now our leaders would know how to engage the public in ways that encourage people to weigh alternative policy choices thoughtfully and intelligently.

Alas, this is not the case. I have spent most of my professional life attempting to distinguish between raw public opinion and considered public judgment. I've written a half-dozen books on how to help the public make the transition from one to the other. After more than a half century of social science research, I have come to the conclusion that our culture is failing badly on this front.

Our society cannot flourish without achieving a sound balance between individual and group interests. Healthy cultures promote that balance through shaping and reinforcing social norms. I had hoped that our culture would now be busy reinforcing a social ethic that honored caring for others, altru-ism, responsibility, service, selflessness, and stewardship.

Instead, our culture celebrates and rewards the crassest forms of narrow self-interest. It is poorly balanced, reinforcing narcissism, and self-seeking rather than the well-being of the larger community.

I don't want to imply that our culture has grown completely lopsided. Most cultural norms still do what they are supposed to do: guide our behavior in work, family, social relations, religion, and the search for political stabil-ity.

There are sick and corrupt cultures in the world. In comparison, our culture in the United States is relatively healthy. The cultural struggles that currently engage us are normal "evolutionary pains."

Our culture may require many more decades to overcome the evolution-ary pains that make it so difficult to balance individual self-fulfillment with societal flourishing.

In the frontispiece to his classic novel *Howards End*, E. M. Forster wrote, "Only connect the prose and the passion and both shall be exalted." The process of breaking out of destructive connections between the prose and the passion of life and forming more positive connections is our major evolution-ary challenge.

In the meantime, you are on your own.

Chapter Forty-Two

Structuring Your Own Philosophy for Living

This semifinal chapter is for readers who want to construct their own philosophy for living but are not quite sure how to get started. My suggestion is to start by answering three questions explored in earlier sections of this book:

1. What do you really care about?
2. What expectations do you place on yourself?
3. How do you personally relate to the great tasks and wicked problems that confront our society?

My guess is that for a long time to come—perhaps several generations—much of the new thinking about philosophy will not come from the academic world but from the American public.

I anticipate a great outpouring of new ideas and values to emerge from the struggles of millions of Americans as they shape a philosophy that snugly fits their lives and helps the nation to confront its wicked problems.

WHAT DO YOU REALLY CARE ABOUT?

The reach of your caring is the ideal place to begin your quest. That reach may encompass family and friends, old neighborhoods, ethnic and religious bonds, core values, ideals, attachments to schools and colleges, your immediate community, "tribe," and patriotism to the nation.

In earlier parts of this book I've emphasized that a key purpose of a philosophy of life is to keep you focused on what really matters. In our brief lifespan, it is not easy to discover the core essentials of life. And it is even more difficult to stay focused on them without distraction. This is why we need culture, representing the cumulative wisdom of human experience.

My suggestion is that you make a written inventory of the full range of people, places, ideas, and things that you care about the most. Select the most beloved concerns and place them on the top of the list.

Then subject the full inventory to the "hypocrisy test."

Most people will automatically put their family on top of the list. And doing so may actually reflect their true feelings. But it may also reflect cultural conformity.

Our culture expects us to put family first, whether we truly mean it or not. For this exercise, however, intellectual honesty is all-important. It's *your* personal philosophy of life. It ought to express your real feelings.

WHAT EXPECTATIONS DO YOU PLACE ON YOURSELF?

To an extraordinary degree, people's expectations of themselves reflect their self-image—how they conceive of themselves in the context of the larger society. And one's individual self-image, in turn, reflects the various ways in which our civilization conceives of the self.

Our Western civilization, still living in the shadow of the Enlightenment, highlights human rationality. But contemporary science paints a contrasting picture. The scientific evidence of what it means to be truly human suggests that

- The nonrational aspects of people dominate the rational ones.
- The human machinery of cognition is inherently error-prone.
- Groupthink and other forms of crooked thinking are the true normal.
- People often don't know their own motives and where their true self-interest lies.
- Evolution is a complex, error-prone process saddling all of us with conflicts and contradictions that are almost impossible to resolve.

To put it bluntly, from a rational perspective humankind seems just a wee bit crazy. In my experience, this is a more accurate portrayal of the human condition than that of the classical economists and other rationalists.

Which portrait—rational or nonrational—is the more accurate one matters a great deal. This is because a conception of the self is the very core of everyone's philosophy for living. To an extraordinary degree, it shapes the expectations we all place on ourselves.

We expect to succeed in today's America because we presuppose that the system, based on merit and equality of opportunity, works rationally as it is supposed to. When we don't succeed, we feel undeservedly guilty, angry, and frustrated. When we do, we undeservedly give ourselves all the credit. But these "rational expectations" are not a valid inference of what we should expect of ourselves in today's world.

We expect the nation—and the world—to work as it should work, and so we underestimate how vast the repair job is for fixing all the serious things that go wrong.

We pay insufficient attention to human nature and expect too much from the systems we have constructed to manage our lives, such as our schools, colleges, businesses, professions, prisons, government agencies, and hospitals. We have too many jails and too few facilities for helping people with mental and emotional problems.

Philosophers Immanuel Kant and Isaiah Berlin wrote about the "crooked timber of humanity." Their metaphor expresses an important truth.

HOW DO YOU PERSONALLY RELATE TO THE GREAT TASKS AND WICKED PROBLEMS THAT CONFRONT OUR SOCIETY?

Each era has its own great tasks to perform and its own wicked problems to confront. Ours is no different, except possibly there are more of them to deal with at the same time.

The great tasks of our era include

Restoring the kind of democracy-friendly capitalism (or its equivalent) that prevailed from the end of WWII to the mid-1970s.

Curbing the extreme individualism of our culture and elevating the importance of caring for the larger community.

Strengthening our social ethos and reviving a strong sense of right versus wrong, as distinct from legal versus illegal.

Upgrading our democracy by strengthening its "by the people" dimension.

Narrowing the social class gap between elites and the general public.

Gaining a better sense of the limits of science as well as its strengths, and acknowledging legitimate nonscientific ways of knowing.

Emphasizing shared frameworks rather than permitting specialist frameworks to prevail; otherwise it becomes too difficult to keep the whole in sight at all times.

Strengthening our system of social mobility.

Repairing our culture so that it doesn't lead to widespread anomie.

Reviving our tradition of compromise and pragmatic problem solving.

Developing better interventions for coping with mental and emotional disorders.

Radically reducing our reliance on imprisonment for managing our social problems.

Encouraging a critical mass of Americans to develop a philosophy of life that focuses on the importance of restoring strong civic virtue to our society.

Every citizen has something to contribute to achieving one or more of these tasks, especially the last one. Each person can select her own special task and do something about it, however modest.

I believe strongly that encouraging Americans to develop their own explicit philosophies for living is necessary to fix the flaws and achieve the tasks listed above.

In looking for remedies, I have emphasized the public's Learning Curve. Paying more attention to it is indispensable to engaging the public.

This will not be easy and will require genuine innovation. If, however, we do learn how to strengthen our democracy by evoking the public's potential for self-governance, we should then find it much easier to develop the will and the skill needed to address many of the other flaws, such as the slippage away from a democracy-friendly form of capitalism, the erosion of our ethical norms, and our reliance on narrow and divisive frameworks that cause us to lose sight of the whole.

In emphasizing the public's role in achieving the freedom that comes with civic virtue, I don't mean to minimize the essential role of our nation's elites. Elite leadership is indispensable to maintaining strong civic virtue in a democracy.

Our elites, despite their positions of authority, are just as subject to crooked thinking as the general public, though for somewhat different reasons. Having so many smart people make so many dumb mistakes may be unique to our times. The kind of specialization that gains mastery over the individual parts of the elephant comes with the trade-off of losing sight of the whole elephant.

I believe that a critical mass of our elites is committed to the ethic of civic virtue and stewardship. If the public were better prepared to deliberate thoughtfully on the great tasks of our times, this segment of our elites would respond constructively.

By and large our elites are neither corrupt nor aristocratic. They simply have fallen out of the habit of consulting with average citizens.

If the public were better prepared to engage the great tasks of our day, the Clintons and Obamas and Bushes and their like would be far more responsive and willing to engage.

So, from the point of view of action, I think it is pragmatically a sounder strategy to focus on the public first and let our elites catch up on their own.

It may not be possible (or desirable) to make the American public into a nation of well-informed experts.

It may not be possible to expand the public's attention span and focus it more sharply on national issues.

It may not be possible (or desirable) to make the public more rational.

But I believe that it is possible—and *very* desirable—to provide the public with the tools it needs to ascend the Learning Curve more surefootedly.

And it is surely possible to encourage individual Americans to acquire philosophies for living that enhance our appreciation of the gift of democracy and self-governance.

Chapter Forty-Three

Some Philosophical Tweets to Live By

"What is the good life? What makes life worth living and gives it meaning?"

I have compressed my response to this ancient Socratic query into twenty tweets. They are the principles that have guided my actions and my life.

They come from four sources. The first is experience—both personal and professional.

My professional experience confirmed for me how important it is when confronted with wicked problems to have a fully engaged public armed with a thoughtful philosophy for living.

My personal experience helped me to develop my strategies for coping, and the pragmatic outlook that goes with it. It also led me to a fuller embrace of intimate relationships.

The second source comes from the findings of science on evolution, human nature, and human cognition. I came to the conclusion that our culture grossly underestimates the primacy of human nature in shaping us as individuals and as a society.

I became awed by the complexity of co-evolution: the need to integrate the timetable of inborn genes (millions of years), language and culture (150,000–200,000 years), and individual development (a paltry 80–90 years).

The work of cognitive psychologists on the brain and on human learning have added a scientific dimension to Freud's insights into the unconscious nature of human thought and motivation, giving far less primacy to reason than the dominant Enlightenment tradition of our intellectual culture.

The third source comes from appreciating the complexities of cultural values. I was genuinely shocked by the realization that our culture—so vital to our stability and well-being—can be thrown badly out of sync with the developmental needs of the individual for generations at a time. The culture can reinforce nutty, truly misguided convictions we acquire about such fun-

193

damentals as marriage, sex, wealth, race, gender, self-expressiveness, sacrifice for others, and self-identity.

Eventually, cultures correct themselves and support genuine human flourishing. But "eventually" may mean lost generations.

The fourth source covers the principles that underlie valid philosophical thinking:

- focusing on the integral nature of the whole and never losing sight of it rather than regarding it merely as the sum of its parts;
- setting explicit value priorities for one's self;
- developing the skill and the will to live by the priorities you have chosen;
- acknowledging your obligations to the larger society;
- making explicit the frameworks underlying your philosophy rather than leaving them tacit;
- deploying the tool of "critique" to identify crooked thinking and distortions in thought;
- living the examined life; and
- bringing an ethic of stewardship to bear on judging both individual lives and entire civilizations.

In the spirit of the times, I have squeezed all of these sources into the following twenty tweets. I present them in no particular order.

DON'T SKIP ANY OF LIFE'S STAGES, EVEN IF OUT OF SEQUENCE.

One of the essential features of human nature is that the focus of our energies shifts as we age. (There is a time for tending one's own garden and a time for nurturing others.) One should be mindful of the seven or so life stages that thinkers like Erik Erikson identify, giving proper attention to the demands of each.

If circumstances cause you to skip a stage, you can come back to it later. Don't automatically reject regression to earlier stages. It can be very good for you. It is never too late.

FIND YOUR OWN WAY TO PRACTICE THE EXAMINED LIFE.

One's spirit needs nourishment. Finding occasions for reflection and thought is as necessary as food and drink. The ability to be self-conscious about life and its meaning is a great gift. But you have to work at it to realize its importance.

MAKE PHILOSOPHICAL THINKING A HABIT.

Put first things first. Never lose sight of the whole. Avoid crooked thinking. Make tacit frameworks explicit. Live the examined life.

CREATE POCKETS OF FREEDOM FOR YOURSELF.

Freedom to make your own choices (and mistakes) is a precondition for American-style individualism. I strongly share this core value of our culture. Throughout my life I have struggled to preserve some degree of freedom of action.

TAKE RISKS WITH YOUR LIFE, AND ACCEPT THE CONSEQUENCES.

Deciding to be a risk taker with one's life is partly a matter of temperament and partly a matter of choice. Both forces converged to make me an inveterate risk taker. It was the right decision for me.

BE SELF-EXPRESSIVE IN WAYS THAT CONTRIBUTE TO OTHERS.

Like many people, I discovered that self-expressiveness was important. It took me a long time to learn what forms of self-expressiveness worked best. Writing books to share my experience with others became a compelling force in my life.

GIVE YOURSELF A BREAK AND MAINTAIN A CERTAIN RESERVE.

The early childhood trauma of my mother's death and family breakup led to a strong need to protect myself. Also: after the age of fifty, I decided to treat every ambiguous comment as a compliment.

AVOID SITUATIONS THAT THREATEN TO CRUSH THE SPIRIT.

The source of this principle was the severity of the threat the humiliating work conditions of the Great Depression posed to my father's spirit. His experience affected me deeply. I have devoted much time and energy to keeping such threats at bay.

RECOGNIZE THAT SUBLIMATIONS ARE SUBSTITUTES.

At every stage of life I have found myself confronting choices between what I truly wanted and what I was obliged to accept as a substitute. Often the substitutes were quite satisfying and genuine lifesavers. But one should see them for what they are, and be prepared to embrace the real thing should the opportunity arise.

ACCEPT THAT YOU ARE LESS RATIONAL THAN YOU THINK YOU ARE.

Cognitively, we are all error-prone and likely to overestimate how much we know. Unconscious childhood motivations drive us to a far greater degree than our culture is willing to acknowledge.

DO NOT FIGHT BEING AN OUTSIDER. RELISH IT!

This principle applies to a minority among us, though a large minority. I was quick to accept outsider status, but slow to relish it. I hope my discovery of its benefits will prove useful to others.

DEPEND ON YOUR OWN STANDARDS.

One downside of adopting an outsider status is that recognition from insiders will be slow in coming. One is better off developing high internal standards and being relentless about meeting them.

ACQUIT WITH HONOR.

Mistakes are inevitable; the important thing is not to leave a mess. However much trouble it may take, it is important to act responsibly and not dump your problems onto others.

RANK INTELLECTUAL HONESTY HIGH ON YOUR CORE VALUES.

For as long as I can remember, intellectual honesty has been important to me. I've avoided many potential defeats by insisting on being honest with myself. I've had to learn to adapt to reality early in life. Self-deception is the enemy of successful adaptation.

BE WILLING TO TAKE A LOT OF RESPONSIBILITY FOR OTHERS.

I've discovered in myself a tendency to take responsibility for others, even when unnecessary or inappropriate. This propensity has caused me a lot of trouble, but I have come to accept it.

PURSUE STEWARDSHIP AS A PERSONAL AS WELL AS A SOCIAL VALUE.

The stewardship commitment to leave any institution better off (or at least not worse) is an important part of my social philosophy. I have discovered that it applies just as much to my own personal and professional relationships.

LEAVE A HERITAGE: DO SOMETHING FOR FUTURE GENERATIONS.

I'm not sure why this desire—so important for many people—is also important for me. It represents an opportunity to transcend the limits of the self and achieve a genuine connection to the world.

GIVE SPECIAL ATTENTION TO THE ACT OF FOUNDING.

I discovered that I greatly enjoy starting new enterprises. The philosopher Hannah Arendt taught me that the act of founding can have an almost sacred quality and is an excellent way to leave a heritage.

TAKE RESPONSIBILITY FOR THE WELL-BEING OF OUR DEMOCRACY.

It takes more than just voting to make democracy work. It takes a responsible, thoughtful public voice. All Americans should be conscious of how precious—and fragile—our democracy is. Participating in making it a more just and effective problem-solving institution is a privilege and ought to be a source of immense personal satisfaction.

NEVER GIVE UP ON SEEKING UNCONDITIONAL LOVE.

In the end I did not give up, and I was right—making for a happy ending, the randomness of life experience notwithstanding.

Constructing your own philosophy of life is a lot of fun, even in the form of tweets.

Notes

1. INTRODUCTION: AMERICA'S WICKED PROBLEMS

1. *Washington Post*, January 28, 2014.
2. *WSJ*, February 1–2, 2014.
3. George Packer, *The Unwinding* (New York: Farrar, Straus and Giroux , 2013), 3.

2. RETROFITTING THE PLUMBING OF DEMOCRACY

1. *The New York Times*/Yankelovich Poll; *TIME*/Yankelovich Poll.

4. FOUR WRONG TURNS

1. Thomas Piketty, *Capital in the Twenty-First Century* (Cambridge, Mass.: Harvard University Press, 2014), 1.
2. State of the Union, January 2014.

6. STRAIGHT AND CROOKED THINKING

1. Daniel Kahneman, *Thinking, Fast And Slow* (New York: Farrar, Strauss and Giroux, 2011), 9–15.
2. Robert Nozick, *The Examined Life, Philosophical Meditations* (New York: Simon and Schuster, 1989), 12.

10. TRANSITIONING TO A THOUGHTFUL PUBLIC — A STRATEGY

1. David Mathews *The Ecology of Democracy* (Dayton, Ohio: Kettering Foundation Press, 2014).

13. PART SCIENCE . . .

1. This is why so many surveys of the era were criticized as "fishing expeditions"—they were fishing around aimlessly because they were not preceded by sound observations and testable hypotheses.

14. PART CIRCUS . . .

1. Ernest Dichter, *Handbook of Consumer Motivations* (New York: McGraw-Hill, 1964).
2. Dichter, *Handbook of Consumer Motivations*.

15. SMART PEOPLE, DUMB MISTAKES

1. Langer Srole et al., *Mental Health in the Metropolis* (New York: McGraw-Hill, 1962).
2. Srole et al., *Mental Health in the Metropolis*, 17.
3. Paul Krugman, *The New York Times Magazine*, September 5, 2011, 36–43.

18. *NEVER* PRESENT MORE THAN ONE IDEA AT A TIME

1. Daniel Yankelovich with David Meer, "Rediscovering Market Segmentation," *Harvard Business Review* (February 2006): 122–31.
2. Yankelovich with Meer, "Rediscovering Market Segmentation," 90.

19. TRACKING THE CULTURAL REVOLUTION

1. *Young Adults: The Threshold Years* (New York: Institute of Life Insurance, 1965), 16.
2. Quoted in *Young Adults*, 21.

20. A SPECIAL BRAND OF REBELLION

1. Daniel Seligman, "A Special Kind of Rebellion," *Fortune Magazine*, January 1969.

21. WHO'S AFRAID OF THE "GENERATION GAP"?

1. An astonishing coincidence: *on the very day* that I wrote these words, I received an e-mail from CBS asking whether I could lay my hands on the original study, conducted more than forty years earlier in 1969! CBS wanted to repeat the study but couldn't find the original questionnaire or results in their files. I was pleased to share my information with them but flabbergasted at the coincidence.
2. *BELL Telephone Magazine*, November/December 1969, 4–7.

22. HIGH-RISK EXPERIMENTS WITHOUT A NET

1. Daniel Yankelovich, *New Rules* (New York: Random House, 1981), 6.
2. Yankelovich, *New Rules*, 7.
3. Yankelovich, *New Rules*, 3.

23. AMERICA TELLS ITSELF A NEW STORY

1. Hannah Arendt, *On Revolution* (New York: Penguin Books, 1963), 28.
2. Arendt, *On Revolution*, 23.
3. Robert Bellah et al., *Habits of the Heart* (New York: Amazon Books, 1985), 25

25. FOUNDING THE PUBLIC AGENDA

1. George E. Vaillant, M.D., *Aging Well* (New York: Little, Brown and Co., 2002), 115.

26. THE ELITIST DOUBLE WHAMMY

1. Daniel Yankelovich, *Moral Leadership in Government* (New York: Public Agenda, 1976), 11.
2. Yankelovich, *Moral Leadership in Government*, 12.
3. Yankelovich, *Moral Leadership in Government*, 13.
4. Yankelovich, *Moral Leadership in Government*, 13.
5. Yankelovich, *Moral Leadership in Government*, 16.
6. Yankelovich, *Moral Leadership in Government*, 15.

28. COMING TO PUBLIC JUDGMENT

1. See *Coming to Public Judgment* (Syracuse, N.Y.: Syracuse University Press, 1991), and *Toward Wiser Public Judgment* (with Will Friedman; Nashville, Tenn.: Vanderbilt University Press, 2010) by the Public Agenda.

29. LOSING THE BATTLE WITH THE NEWS MEDIA

1. Daniel Yankelovich, "Farewell to 'President Knows Best,'" *Foreign Affairs* 57, no. 3 (1979).
2. Yankelovich, Skelly and White, *The Mushiness Index: A Refinement in Public Policy Techniques*, March 1981.

31. DINNER WITH QUINE

1. Willard Van Orman Quine, *Mathematical Logic* (Cambridge, Mass.: Harvard University Press, 1940).

32. HOW SCIENTISM NEARLY DEVOURED PHILOSOPHY

1. Alfred North Whitehead, *Science and the Modern World* (New York: Free Press, 1925), 2.
2. Quoted in Kenneth Seeskin, "Never Speculate, Never Explain," *The American Scholar*, 1980, 22.
3. Hans Reichenbach, *Rise of Scientific Philosophy* (Berkeley: University of California Press, 1951).
4. Richard Rorty, "Philosophy in America Today," in *The Consequences of Pragmatism* (Minneapolis: University of Minnesota Press, 1982).
5. Rorty, "Philosophy in America Today," 19.
6. Richard Bernstein, *Pragmatism, Pluralism, and the Healing of Wounds*, presidential address to the Eastern Division of the American Philosophical Association (Newark, Del.: American Philosophical Association, 1988), 333, 337, and 338.
7. Bernstein, *Pragmatism*, 333.
8. Seeskin, "Never Speculate, Never Explain."
9. Seeskin, "Never Speculate, Never Explain," 21.

33. MY WRONG MAP PROBLEM

1. Sigmund Koch, *Psychology: A Study of a Science*, vol. 7 (New York: McGraw-Hill, 1959–), 45.
2. Cited in the article on "Behaviorism" in the *Stanford Encyclopedia of Philosophy*, rev. ed. (Stanford, Calif.: Stanford University, July 2007), 5.

34. A LOOK AT EXISTENTIALISM

1. Rollo May, Ernest Angel, and Henri F. Ellenberger, eds., *Existence* (New York: Basic Books, 1958).

35. FINDING A BETTER FRAMEWORK

1. Daniel Yankelovich, "The Impact of Existentialism on Psychology," presented to the Massachusetts Psychological Association, February 25, 1965.

36. APPLYING PHILOSOPHY TO PSYCHOANALYSIS

1. Sigmund Freud, *Outline of Psychoanalysis* (London: Hogarth Press, 1964), 17.
2. Ludwig Binswagner, *Selected Papers*, ed. Jacob Needleman (New York: Basic Books, 1927).

37. "EGO AND INSTINCT" IN RETROSPECT

1. Avery Weisman, *The Existentialist Core of Psychoanalysis* (Boston: Little, Brown, 1965).
2. Daniel Yankelovich and William Barrett, *Ego and Instinct* (New York: Random House, 1970).

38. THE MIND-SET OF THE IRON CAGE: PRYING IT OPEN

1. Daniel Yankelovich, unpublished lectures.

39. DON'T FIGHT HUMAN NATURE!

1. Steven Pinker, *The Blank Slate—The Modern Denial of Human Nature* (New York: Viking, 2003).
2. Quoted as an appendix to Pinker's *The Blank Slate*. See pages 435–39.

40. CO-EVOLUTION

1. George E. Vaillant, *Spiritual Evolution* (New York: Broadway Books, 2008), 41.
2. Vaillant, *Spiritual Evolution*, 44.
3. Daniel Kahneman, *Thinking, Fast And Slow* (New York: Farrar, Strauss and Giroux, 2011), 9–10.
4. Kahneman, *Thinking, Fast And Slow*, 4.

41. CULTURE IS INESCAPABLE . . .

1. For example, the creation of a living cell with manmade, artificial DNA, using ingredients (amino acids) not found in life on earth (Scripps Research Institute, May 8, 2014).

Bibliography

Arendt, Hannah. *On Revolution*. New York: Penguin Books, 1963.

Bellah, Robert, et al. *Habits of the Heart*. New York: Amazon Books, 1985.

Binswagner, Ludwig. *Selected Papers*. Ed. Jacob Needleman. New York: Basic Books, 1927.

Kahneman, Daniel. *Thinking, Fast and Slow*. New York: Farrar, Strauss and Giroux, 2011.

Koch, Sigmund. *Psychology: A Study of a Science*, vol. 7. New York: McGraw-Hill, 1959–.

Mathews, David. *The Ecology of Democracy*. Dayton, Ohio: Kettering Foundation Press, 2014.

May, Rollo, and Ernest Angel and Henri F. Ellenberger, editors. *Existence*. New York: Basic Books, 1958.

Nozick, Robert. *The Examined Life, Philosophical Meditations*. New York: Simon and Schuster, 1989.

Packer, George. *The Unwinding*. New York: Farrar, Straus and Giroux, 2013.

Piketty, Thomas. *Capital in the Twenty-First Century*. Cambridge, Mass.: Harvard University Press, 2014.

Pinker, Steven. *The Blank Slate—The Modern Denial of Human Nature*. New York: Viking, 2003.

Quine, Willard Van Orman. *Mathematical Logic*. Cambridge, Mass.: Harvard University Press, 1940.

Reichenbach, Hans. *Rise of Scientific Philosophy*. Berkeley: University of California Press, 1951.

Rorty, Richard. "Philosophy in America Today." In *The Consequences of Pragmatism*. Minneapolis: University of Minnesota Press, 1982.

Seeskin, Kenneth. "Never Speculate, Never Explain." *The American Scholar*, 1980, 22.

Seligman, Daniel. "A Special Kind of Rebellion." *Fortune Magazine*, January 1969.

Srole, Langer, et al. *Mental Health in the Metropolis*. New York: McGraw-Hill, 1962.

Valliant, George E. *Aging Well*. New York: Little, Brown and Co., 2002.

———. *Spiritual Evolution*. New York: Broadway Books, 2008.

Weisman, Avery. *The Existentialist Core of Psychoanalysis*. Boston: Little, Brown, 1965.

Yankelovich, Daniel. *BELL Telephone Magazine*, November/December 1969.

———. *Coming to Public Judgment*. Syracuse, N.Y.: Syracuse University Press, 1991.

———. "Farewell to 'President Knows Best.'" *Foreign Affairs* 57, no. 3 (1979).

———. "The Impact of Existentialism of Psychology." Presented to the Massachusetts Psychological Association, February 25, 1965.

———. *Moral Leadership in Government*. New York: Public Agenda, 1976.

———. "New Criteria for Market Segmentation." *Harvard Business Review*, 1964.

———. *New Rules*. New York: Random House, 1981.

Yankelovich, Daniel, with David Meer. "Rediscovering Market Segmentation." *Harvard Business Review*, February 2006, 122–31.

Yankelovich, Daniel, with Will Friedman. *Toward Wiser Public Judgment*. Nashville, Tenn.: Vanderbilt University Press, 2010.

Yankelovich, Daniel, and William Barrett. *Ego and Instinct*. New York: Random House, 1970.

Yankelovich, Skelly and White. *The Mushiness Index: A Refinement in Public Policy Techniques*. March 1981.

Young Adults: The Threshold Years. New York: Institute of Life Insurance, 1965.

Index

208 *Index*

About the Author

Daniel Yankelovich attributes his successful career to his willingness to think independently and not automatically accept the familiar way of doing things. He discovered that it often made sense to cut across traditional boundaries. He learned to move easily between worlds—profit-making and not-for-profit, the world of the writer and that of the doer, the enterprise and academic worlds. He was, he says, agreeably surprised to learn how many practical advantages the examined life gives one.

FACTUAL BACKGROUND INFORMATION

Corporate director: six major corporate boards, including CBS, the Meredith Company, and USWest

Trustee: five nonprofit boards, including Brown University, the Kettering Foundation, and the University of California at San Diego (UCSD)

Author: eleven books including, *New Rules*, *The Magic of Dialogue*, and *Coming to Public Judgment*

Founder: five companies and nonprofits, including The Public Agenda; Yankelovich, Skelly and White; the *New York Times*/Yankelovich Poll

Board chairman: six organizations, including the Educational Testing Service (ETS), the Armenian Advisory Committee (Columbia University), the Society for the Advancement of Socioeconomics

Honors: the Exceptionally Distinguished Achievement Award of the American Association of Public Opinion Research, the Distinguished Graduate of the Year award from the Boston Latin School, the Parlin Award for pioneering work in marketing research, honorary doctorates from several universities

University lecturing: Harvard, NYU, the New School for Social Research, Tufts Medical School, the University of California at Irvine

Philanthropy: endowed the Yankelovich Professorship in Social Thought and the Yankelovich Center for Social Science Research at UCSD

Education: undergraduate degree from Harvard University, graduate Studies at Harvard and the Sorbonne